ISBN 1-877292-93-1

DELIVER A SERVICE
TO CUSTOMERS

by

Melanie Bhagat

Software Publications

Deliver a service to customers

Author: Melanie Bhagat LLB

Editor: Cheryl Price T.Dip.WP, T.Dip.T.

ISBN: 1-877292-93-1

Disclaimer

Publishers – Software Publications Pty Ltd (ABN 75 078 026 150)

Head Office – Sydney
Unit 10, 171 Gibbes Street
Chatswood NSW 2067
Australia

Web Address
www.softwarepublications.com

Branches

Adelaide, Brisbane, Melbourne, Perth and Auckland

Table of Contents

Introduction to Delivering a Service to Customers 1
  Why are these questions important? 1
Who Are Your Customers? 3
  Customers can be *internal* or *external*..3
  Customers can be *individuals* or *organisations*..3
    Internal work colleagues...4
    External members of the public 4
    External organisations or agencies...6
    A combination of the above 6
  Examples of customers 7
Identifying Customer Needs 8
Personality 9
  General 9
  Empathy...9
  Thoughtfulness..9
  Tact...9
  Loyalty...10
  Discretion 10
  Have a good attitude 10
  How to improve your attitude 10
  Mature judgement 11
  Versatility 11
  Objectivity 11
  Initiative...11
Self-Confidence 14
  Developing self-confidence 14
Body Language...16
  What is body language?...16
  Why is body language so important?..16
  How do we communicate with body language? 17
  Table: What your body language is saying when your mouth is shut!..............................18
Effective Listening Skills...21
  The four steps to effective listening 21
  Becoming a better listener...21
  Ineffective listening - What *not* to do...23
Being an Active Listener...24
  Active listening techniques 24
    Encouraging 25
    Rephrasing...25
    Summarising 25
Asking Questions 27
  Closed questions...27
  Open questions..28
  Leading questions 29
  Double questions 29
Who Should Help Customers? 32
Helping Customers Yourself..32
Referring Customers 33
  When should customers be referred?...33
  Who should customers be referred to?...34
  How to refer customers 36
  Customers who may not want to be referred 36
Good Customer Relations...37
  Be prompt 37
  Your manner and attitude 37

Your voice.. 37
Use the customer's name 37
Special tips when dealing with customers *on the telephone*............................ 38
Good telephone answering technique 38
What Products and Services Can You Offer to Your Customers?......................... 40
Gathering information.. 41
Helping Customers Choose the Right Service or Product 42
Involve the customer... 42
Use appropriate body language 42
Use your listening and questioning skills 43
Making the final choice.. 45
Your approach 45
Delivering the Service 46
Your organisation's requirements... 46
Where to find information on your organisation's requirements 47
Helpful resources 50
What services will customers need? 51
Assisting customers correctly... 52
Giving Information to Customers 55
Your voice and language 55
What information to give 55
Keeping listeners' attention 55
To finish 55
Prioritising Customers' Requests 57
Considerations 57
Urgency 57
A chain of information 58
Be honest... 58
Aids to prioritising your time 58
Standard turnaround times... 59
Examples of turnaround times set by organisations 59
What Other Needs Do Customers Have? 60
Understanding customer needs 61
Extra needs... 63
Assisting customers with extra needs.. 63
Enhancing the Quality of Your Service.. 64
Adding value to your service 65
Further examples on enhancing the quality of service...................................... 69
Scenario 1: A furniture sales outlet... 69
Scenario 2: Internet beauty products service.. 69
Scenario 3: Computer repair centre... 70
Scenario 4: Hotel... 70
Handling Complaints.. 71
How not to deal with a complaint.. 71
How do complaints arise?... 72
The basics in dealing with complaints 73
Listen and gather information.. 73
Interpersonal skills 74
Responding to the customer 75
Remedying problems 76
Difficult Situations and Problem Customers 79
Feedback.. 80
Learn from your experiences... 80
Summary 82
Revision.. 84
Skills Test 85
Revision Answers 89

Introduction to Delivering a Service to Customers

Delivering a service means performing the role that your organisation has employed you to perform. It could involve any of the following:

- Selling a product

- Providing training in management skills

- Plumbing in a washing machine

- Making beds in a hotel

- Dealing cards at a casino ...... the list is endless!

If your job involves delivering a service to clients, customers, visitors or colleagues, then you are in the 'front line' of your organisation. This means that you are a direct link between your organisation and its customers – the people who keep it in business. You are the person whom customers deal with, and so it is from your appearance, attitude, behaviour and standard of service that customers will form their opinion of your organisation.

If the customers are not treated well, they may well take their business to a company that will provide them with better service. Obviously, if an organisation loses too many customers, it risks getting a bad reputation and – eventually – going out of business.

Therefore it is vital for all employees who deliver a service to customers to deliver it well, and keep the customers happy. This workbook is designed to help you learn how to do this.

Some questions that we will look at are the following:

- Who are your customers?

- Which products and services can you offer your customers?

- What do your customers need from you?

Why are these questions important?

Put yourself in the position of a customer and consider the following situations.

- The manager of the local steak house keeps ringing you up to offer you a discounted meal despite you telling him many times that you are a vegetarian,

- The secretary of your tennis club assures you that your subscription fee includes swimming, but you discover the club doesn't even have a pool, or

- Your doctor doesn't listen to a word you said and prescribes cough medicine for your aching knee.

I expect that you wouldn't be very impressed with any of these services and wouldn't form a good opinion of the people that had served you or the organisation that they represent.

Similarly, your own customers will come away with a poor impression of you and your organisation if you target the wrong people, fail to deliver what they need or don't know your own services well enough to be able to help them.

As customers, we have certain wants and needs from people who provide services to us – and if these are not met, we are disappointed.

Taking the examples above,

- The vegetarian would be more interested in a different restaurant than a steakhouse (note that the steak house manager didn't know who his customers were),

- The swimmer should have been advised to join a swimming club not a tennis club (note that the secretary didn't know what services the tennis club offered), and

- The patient needed a knee examination not cough mixture (note that the doctor didn't know what her patient needed from her).

This book aims to help you answer the three questions above - the *who*, *which* and *what* of delivering a service to customers – so that *you* can deliver a great service to your customers.

Along the way we will discuss many other related topics. You can chart your progress through the book, by following this chart.

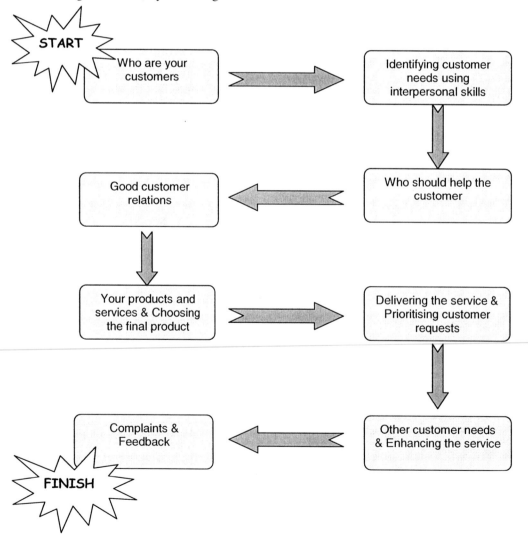

Who Are Your Customers?

Your customers are all the people that you deal with in your working life.

Some examples are obvious, for example,

- A hairdresser's customers are customers who want their hair cut, permed or coloured.

- A dental nurse's customers are patients who attend the dental surgery.

- A supermarket cashier's customers are customers at the shop who bring items to the till.

- An animal trainer's customers are pet owners who bring their pets in for training.

However, these people may have other customers who may not immediately be so obvious, eg

- The hairdresser may have trainees working part-time in the salon while they learn the trade. These trainees are also customers.

- The dental nurse may liaise with dental organisations or other surgeries to keep abreast of new techniques – these organisations would also be customers.

> Think about a sub-editor on a magazine and the IT manager in a large company who trouble-shoots staff's computer problems. Who are their customers? We will return to this question after looking at customers in more detail.

Customers can be *internal* or *external*

- Customers can be "internal" (or "in-house"), which means that they come from within the same organisation as us (eg colleagues in our department or in other departments, branches or regional offices).

- Customers can be "external" (or "out-of-house"), which means that they come from outside our organisation.

Customers can be *individuals* or *organisations*

- Customers can be individual members of the public, such as a shopper or an office worker.

- Customers can be groups, organisations or agencies, such as Government Departments, local bodies, fundraising groups or pressure groups.

Let's take a closer look at these categories.

Internal work colleagues

Some people may spend most of their time dealing with other workers in the same organisation, for example

- a mailroom worker might spend a lot of time collecting and delivering post within the organisation,

- a chef might work with the kitchen staff and the maitre d'.

These customers are **internal, individual members of our organisation**.

Are you wondering why our internal colleagues are called 'customers'? It is because employees are very valuable to a company, and it is therefore essential that they are respected and treated well at work, by other work colleagues as well as by managers.

It costs a company a lot of money to find, recruit and train an employee. Once trained, an employee has invaluable knowledge about the best and most efficient way to do their job.

If they do not enjoy their job, they may well leave - taking all their skills and knowledge with them, and leaving the company to start another expensive round of recruitment to fill their shoes.

Exercise 1

Think of two examples of workers who mainly have internal customers.

1 ....

2 ....

External members of the public

Some employees may have a lot of contact with members of the public who are buying their goods or using their services, for example

- a supermarket worker,

- a doctor,

- an electrician,

- a waitress,

- a nurse,

- a hotel doorman,

- an airline steward/ess.

These customers are **external, individual members of the public**.

External customers are also essential to organisations. It is external customers who buy our services or products, which keeps the organisation functioning. In effect, external customers pay our wages for us.

Exercise 2

Think of two examples of employees who have external customers.

1 ....

2 ....

Remember that *anyone* we deal with at work is a customer and we must behave towards them all professionally. Test your own professionalism by imagining yourself in the following scenario.

Scenario: Treating both internal and external customers well

There was a break-in at your place of work yesterday. You were away from work sick yesterday. Today you are very busy catching up with client orders, a lot of which are now urgent. The security manager comes round to tell you that the police would like a meeting with everyone in your department in the Board Room in one hour's time. Do you:

(a) Assume that because you were away from work yesterday you are exempt from attending the meeting.

(b) Go to the meeting and let your client orders wait until tomorrow – a break-in is more important than orders.

(c) Consult with your manager to get extra help so that all orders can be dispatched today, while still giving you time to attend the meeting.

Response (a) is unsatisfactory because the security manager has requested that *everyone* attends the police meeting. You may have valuable information that can assist the police in investigating the break-in. The security manager is an internal customer and internal customers should be afforded the same quality of response as external customers.

Response (b) is unsatisfactory because your clients (external customers) will be relying on receiving their goods. If they do not receive them when they expect to, they will begin not to trust your organisation and may go elsewhere to purchase their goods.

Response (c) is satisfactory because you have found a way to fulfil both of your immediate responsibilities. If your manager cannot provide extra help, other avenues open to you would be to ask the security manager if it is possible for you to meet with the police *after* you have completed your orders. Alternatively it may be appropriate to dispatch only the urgent client orders today, attend the meeting and then complete the non-time critical orders tomorrow.

External organisations or agencies

Some employees may deal with external agencies or organisations rather than individuals, for example

- a product manufacturer may deal with consumer groups and safety organisations,

- a Member of Parliament may deal with employment unions, constituency groups and charities.

These customers are **external, agency** customers.

A combination of the above

Most employees have to deal with a huge variety of customers – both internal and external, and both individuals and organisations, for example,

- a receptionist will greet guests and also assist staff members,

- a head waiter will deal both with the waiting staff and with diners,

- a charity administrator will deal with members of the public who wish to donate money and also government bodies, which set rules and procedures for charities.

Exercise 3

Consider the following workers and tick which group their customers would come from predominantly (customers may come from more than one group).

	Work Colleagues	Individual members of the public	Other organisations
Animal Welfare Charity volunteer helper	☐	☐	☐
Caretaker for office building	☐	☐	☐
Travel agent	☐	☐	☐
Estate agent	☐	☐	☐
Consumer Pressure Group administrator	☐	☐	☐

Exercise 4

Note down two customers that you deal with in your job – or in the job you hope to get in the future - and categorise them as internal, external or agency.

Your job/ideal job is: ....

1 ....

2 ....

Examples of customers

Let's return to the question we asked on page 3 above.

> Think about a sub-editor on a magazine and the IT manager in a large company who trouble-shoots computer problems. Who are their customers?

We have made some suggestions about possible customers below. Note down on the right what type of customer the employee is dealing with in each instance.

Exercise 5	Internal/External/Agency
Sub-editor He may liaise with authors to arrange an appropriate date for their work to be submitted. He may deal with picture libraries to obtain appropriate photos to accompany stories. He may pass invoices to the accounts department for payment. He may have a weekly meeting with other sub-editors on the magazine to discuss story ideas. He may contact recruitment agencies to obtain temporary secretarial support when admin staff are sick.	
IT manager She may research, cost and order appropriate software from local distributors. She may arrange with local charities to provide them with out-of-date computer equipment free of charge when the company has no more use for it. She may give short training courses to company staff in the lunch hour on software updates.	

Identifying Customer Needs

In order to deliver a good service, we need to know what customers **need** from us. To find out what customers need, we use our 'interpersonal skills'.

Interpersonal skills are skills in dealing with other people. For example, how we *listen*, how we *understand*, how we *give information*, whether we are *friendly, positive, confident*, etc, are all interpersonal skills. Good interpersonal skills are vital in accurately identifying what our customers need.

Interpersonal skills include:

- Your personality,

- Your self-confidence,

- Your body language,

- Your ability to listen effectively,

- Your ability to double-check that you have understood correctly, and

- Your ability to question effectively to gain information.

Let's look at these different interpersonal skills in more detail.

Personality

In our home life, we may get grumpy or annoyed with people. However at work, we must avoid being negative towards our customers. After all, our external customers keep us in business and our internal customers have professional jobs to do, as we do, and we need to work with them on a day-to-day basis. Nobody is perfect but to progress in the workplace there are certain personality traits that are worth developing or enhancing.

For example, if an external customer approaches us in the workplace and is quite clearly angry about something, it is a great skill to be able to calm them down and get them to talk to you rationally. Ultimately, this will create a much more productive relationship than being angry back – and it could win you a customer for life.

The following traits are some key personal qualities that will help you get along with customers - work colleagues and external customers alike.

General

- Be someone to whom people instinctively respond with pleasure

- Have a ready smile that expresses genuine warmth and interest without being too effusive, as this can seem insincere

- Enjoy meeting and talking with all sorts of people

- Stay cool in chaotic situations

- Be efficient without being bossy

Empathy

- Sense how someone else is feeling - it will help you to understand why a customer is nervous, angry or aggressive

- Show an interest in others rather than in yourself

Thoughtfulness

- Listen attentively to what people say, and *then* offer relevant suggestions

- Have a genuine concern for others' needs and feelings

Tact

- Smooth over difficult situations

- Know when to make helpful suggestions and when to draw back

- Make someone who has made a mistake feel better about themselves

Loyalty

- Be loyal to your company. Never discuss company policy with outsiders

- Be loyal to your colleagues. Do not discuss their private lives with others, and don't gossip

Discretion

- Keep company/staff secrets. A careless remark could tip off a competitor or create ill feeling

- Know when to side-step seemingly innocuous requests for information and be sure that your answer won't divulge information that your company would not want released

Have a good attitude

- Your attitude will shape your life

- The right attitude can make you a winner in everything you do

- Enthusiasm spreads energy, happiness, exhilaration, and is catching!

How to improve your attitude

☑ Be enthusiastic and willing even if you don't want to do something - you might end up enjoying it after all.

☑ Smile at people - you might be surprised how many smile back.

☑ Thank people for what they do for you - when did you last thank a member of your family for doing a routine job, eg cooking breakfast, doing your ironing?

☑ Replace the "What's in it for me?" attitude with "How can I help?"

☑ Lighten up: laugh at yourself; laugh with others. Don't take yourself too seriously but do take others seriously and take your job seriously.

☑ Look for the good in people and look for the opportunity to praise people.

☑ Expect positive results.

☑ Assume responsibility for your success - no excuses. Action is the key.

Mature judgement

- Know when to deal with a problem yourself and when to pass it on

- Admit when you don't know something – it is much better than bluffing and being caught out

Versatility

- Be flexible and able to adapt easily to many different situations

- Be able to act competently in an emergency or a rush period

Objectivity

- Keep your personal likes and dislikes to yourself. Don't let them affect work decisions

- Recognise which tasks are crucial and which are not. Carry out important tasks first, rather than just the jobs you happen to like best

Initiative

- Prioritise effectively

- Act wisely on your own without having to be told what to do

- Write reminders to yourself (in a diary or on a To Do list) if you cannot remember to do certain tasks. Also, write down procedures so you don't have to keep asking other staff members to repeat instructions that they have previously given you

---

Exercise 6

Circle which personality trait would be **lacking** if I did the following things.

1   Told an external customer that my organisation was going to lay people off.

         VERSATILITY   OBJECTIVITY   DISCRETION

2   Told my colleague bluntly that she had done her job very badly.

         TACT   INITIATIVE   GOOD ATTITUDE

3   Did my routine jobs first thing in the morning because my manager had forgotten to tell me to do the urgent jobs first.

         THOUGHTFULNESS   MATURE JUDGEMENT   INITIATIVE

Consider the following conversation. It goes very badly for Carl. Read the personality traits on the previous pages again and rewrite the conversation yourself. Hopefully it will go better for you than it did for Carl!

Carl's Conversation

Customer: I need to exchange this frying pan – I fried an egg and now it has a hole in it!

Carl: You must be a terrible cook – I expect you had the heat up too high. It's your error rather than the pan's fault. Anyway we don't give refunds.

Customer: I want to exchange it actually. I hardly think this could be caused just by having the heat up - I think the pan must be faulty. Who can I talk to about that?

Carl: It's usually Customer Services, but they are short-staffed because lots of staff are leaving. They won't have time for something as trivial as this, right now. They are far too busy to be bothered.

Customer: If everyone is leaving, then your company really ought to make the effort to recruit more people.

Carl: The trouble is we don't pay good enough wages, so it's very difficult.

Your Conversation

Customer: I need to exchange this frying pan – I fried an egg and now it has a hole in it!

You: ....

....

Customer: ....

....

You: ....

....

Customer: ....

....

You: ....

....

Note the qualities that you used here: ....

....

Exercise 8

How do you rate yourself? Under each sub-heading, circle the comment that is most applicable to you and then add up your points score.

Friendliness			
I enjoy meeting and talking to new people. I always have a smile at work. *(3 points)*	I like to chat to people – except when I'm having a really bad day. *(2 points)*	If I have spare time, I'll chat but if not I tend to avoid people. *(1 point)*	Smiling only encourages people to waste time. *(0 points)*

Tact			
When I point out that someone has made a mistake, I also comment on their good points too. *(3 points)*	If someone has made a mistake, I tell them straight out but don't dwell too much on it. *(2 points)*	People rely on my straight-talking – I don't aim to upset people, but some people don't like my bluntness. *(1 point)*	I tell everyone about other people's mistakes and have a good laugh about them. *(0 points)*

Attitude			
Even if I don't want to do something, I do it willingly as I learn a lot from those jobs. *(3 points)*	I will do jobs that I don't want to do, but I prefer not to. *(2 points)*	If I'm bullied into it, I'll do horrible jobs, but I'm good at getting out of doing them. *(1 point)*	I don't do anything I don't want to do. *(0 points)*

Loyalty			
I am privileged to know private information, and I won't disclose it without authorisation. *(3 points)*	I'm generally very good at keeping secrets, but I have been known to let something slip out. *(2 points)*	I often tell other people things about the company but only if I think they can keep it private too. *(1 point)*	Some information that I get given is just too juicy to keep to myself. *(0 points)*

Versatility			
I enjoy doing different tasks, and will often volunteer for them – I learn lots and it's interesting. *(3 points)*	I will do new things if asked, but I prefer to do what I know. *(2 points)*	I try to keep out of the way when new tasks are being doled out. *(1 point)*	If it's not in my job description, I won't do it. *(0 points)*

Mature Judgement			
I tell customers when I don't have the authority to do what they want, but I always find them someone who does. *(3 points)*	I call my manager over once it becomes obvious to the customer that I don't know what I am talking about! *(2 points)*	I usually string the customer along for a bit because they will think I'm very junior if I have to say I can't help them. *(1 point)*	If I can't do something, I tell the customer I can, and then just 'lose' their request on my desk somewhere. *(0 points)*

Write your total here: ☐

If you scored 18 points, well done. If not, there is definitely room for improvement.

Self-Confidence

Self-confidence is an *attitude of mind*. Self-confidence is very important, as you might be very highly trained in work skills but fail to get the job because you lack the confidence to sell yourself at interview. You need not only to *have* skills but to *show* others that you have them too.

Self-confidence can help you by making you believe that you are good enough to achieve your goals – whether it is to get a new job, be promoted, move to a different department or learn new skills.

Developing self-confidence

- Pay attention to your grooming and personal presentation. Dress for the job you want, not the job you have!

- Take pride in your work. Do your work to the best of your ability then take a little extra care.

- Project a confident image. Speak clearly rather than mumbling and watch your posture. Don't be afraid to speak up and make suggestions where appropriate.

- Be a solutions person rather than a problem person. Suggest how you can put things right rather than just pointing out what is wrong.

- Stretch yourself. Try and push yourself to do a difficult thing each day, eg if you are shy, chat to someone in the company that you haven't spoken to before. If you don't like public speaking, offer to make a presentation on some aspect of your job that others may not know about but might find helpful. You might surprise yourself and find that it's not that difficult after all. Usually the thought of doing these things is much worse than actually doing them!

Exercise 9

Think of a skill that you don't have or something that you don't like doing but that would be helpful in your workplace (or ideal workplace). Write it here. Jot down brief notes of how you could learn this skill or overcome your fear. You may want to get ideas from a friend or teacher too.

....

....

....

....

....

....

Practical point – Running a customer focus group

If you are dealing with customers, you may at some point need to find out more information about how customers view your organisation, how they view your products or services, and how you could improve the service you give to your customers.

The best way to answer these questions is to talk directly to customers themselves. To do this you could hold a Customer Focus Group in which you ask a specially selected group of customers specific questions about your service.

Define what your Customer Focus Group will discuss tightly

Don't have too wide a remit for your Focus Group. For example, if you work for a publishing house and publish travel books, children's books and books for accountants – don't attempt to have a single Focus Group which covers all your books. At best the accountants won't have a view on your children's books range, and at worst they will become very bored and 'switch off' from your meeting.

Who to invite

It is important to have a broad range of customers so that you get a good cross-section of viewpoints. For example you should ask both long-term customers and customers that have recently starting buying from you. Also, don't shy away from customers who have been critical of the organisation or your service – these customers are the ones that can provide most help when it comes to making improvements.

Agenda

To get the most out of the Focus Group, write out an agenda before the meeting and circulate it to the attendees. Ask the attendees if there is anything they would like added to the agenda (this makes them feel involved and gives you some prior notice of topics that may arise). Make sure you leave plenty of time at the end of the meeting for 'Any other business', which are other issues that attendees want to raise.

Encourage your customers to talk

Perhaps have a coffee session before the meeting starts to break the ice. Ensure that everyone knows who everyone else is - you could provide name plates or you could ask everyone to introduce themselves to the rest of the group.

Remember that you are there to learn

Your Focus Group is being held so that YOU can gain information from it. To do this effectively your customers must feel that they are being listened to – otherwise they will clam up and be reluctant to speak. Therefore, it is important to give your customers a chance to speak critically as well as positively. If customers are critical of something that your organisation had done, don't jump in to explain your side of things. Let them speak. You should take their comments on board and make notes.

Follow-up

Give your customers a 'reward' for their help. You may want to give them a voucher for your service or product.

Ensure that customers know that what they have told you is valued - make sure that they are thanked and kept informed of what changes occur as a result of your meeting.

Body Language

What is body language?

We are all trained in the use of speech to communicate what we mean in a way that other people will understand. Most of the time, others understand what we mean. In a telephone conversation, we communicate through speech alone but in a face-to-face meeting, part of the communication is carried on in a non-verbal form, often called *body language*.

The key aspects of body language are:

1   Eye contact

2   Posture

3   Body position

4   Personal space

5   Actions and gestures

6   Facial expressions

Why is body language so important?

There are two principal reasons why body language is important:

1   People *remember* more of what they see than what they hear.

2   People tend to *believe* what they see rather than what they hear because body language is seen as being more honest. When words and body language say different things, we tend to believe the body language and doubt the words.

Example

Compare the expressions of the following two waiters.

 Diners are more likely to want to talk to the waiter on the right. They might ask him about specials and wines. They'll probably stay longer, eat and drink more and spend more money.

How do we communicate with body language?

Take the position of your body as an example.

➢ You can face towards the speaker, making eye contact. Alternatively, you may face to the side but have one foot forward pointing towards the speaker. These signs indicate that you are interested in what the speaker has to say and want to hear more.

➢ You can lean backwards or turn to the side with no feet facing the speaker. This has very negative implications and shows a lack of interest – or boredom. If you have your arms crossed or are looking down towards the ground, this creates even more of a barrier between you and the speaker.

➢ You can turn away from the speaker during the conversation or – worst of all – turn your back on the speaker and address him/her over your shoulder. This is very negative and shows that you have lost interest in the conversation and want to get away.

Consider the following situations.

How do you interpret this body language? Do you agree with our comments?

	We suggest:
	These two friends are facing towards each other and are making friendly eye contact. They are looking at each other but probably breaking eye contact every few seconds so as not to be too intense. This is the ideal way to address other people. It is friendly and interested but not threatening or aggressive.
	This pair of eyes is guaranteed to make the other person uncomfortable! Staring can be aggressive and unpleasantly intense.

Take a look at the following table to see how aspects of our body language can be either positive or negative.

Table: What your body language is saying when your mouth is shut!

1 Eye contact

Positive		Negative
Making frequent eye contact indicates interest.		Staring will make people uncomfortable and can seem threatening.
		Avoiding eye contact will make you appear shifty and/or bored and disinterested.

2 Posture

Positive		Negative
A relaxed posture indicates no major barriers to communication.		A tense body can indicate concern with the topic or in dealing with the other person.

3 Body position

Positive		Negative
Facing forward, with shoulders and feet facing the other party, or body facing to one side, but with one foot pointing towards the other person, shows interest and desire to listen.		Body and both feet facing to the side indicates disinterest and desire to get away. Turning one's back shows great keenness to be elsewhere.

4 Personal space

Positive		Negative
Leaning closer to reduce the distance between two people, indicates growing interest.		Leaning away can indicate a lack of interest or agreement with what is being said. Encroaching on personal space is threatening.

5 Actions		
Positive		**Negative**
Uncrossed arms and hands open (palms up or otherwise visible to the other person) are signs of openness.		Arms folded in front creates a barrier and can express resistance to what is being said.
Nodding agreement signals agreement, interest and understanding.		Fidgeting, yawning or being distracted is usually a sign of boredom, nervousness or impatience. The other person is talking too much or in too much technical detail.
Taking notes shows interest and involvement.		Biting nails or nervous tapping with the fingers indicates nervousness and worry or concern at what is being said.
Smiling/adding humour signals a warm personal relationship.		A hand over one's mouth or leaning on one's elbow with the chin in the hand can communicate boredom.
Using the hands to gesture indicates involvement in the conversation and openness to the other person.		Trying to interrupt what the other person is saying or opening one's mouth frequently as if to speak, shows impatience.

6 Facial expressions		
Positive		**Negative**
Smiling shows warmth and interest and encourages the speaker to continue with what they are saying.		Wrinkled brow and frowning indicates non-agreement with what is being said or uncomfortableness with speaker's opinions.

Answer the following questions.

1   Why is verbal communication important to a hairdresser?

....

....

2   What other aspects of a customer might a hairdresser look at to gain information about their client's style?

....

....

3   Give two examples of positive verbal communication and two examples of negative verbal communication.   What do they tell you about the other person?

Positive

a   ....

....

b   ....

....

Negative

a   ....

....

b   ....

....

Effective Listening Skills

You need to *listen* in order to find out what customers want from you so that you can provide them with the service that they need. If you try to guess you may get it wrong and make the customer feel that you are more interested in your own opinions than theirs. There are four stages to the listening process.

The four steps to effective listening

1   *Hear*. At this stage, you simply pay attention to make sure you have heard the message. Don't interrupt the speaker or put limitations on your listening time, or the speaker will get the impression that you are not interested in what they are saying.

2   *Interpret*. Decide what the speaker means. Failure to interpret the speaker's words correctly frequently leads to misunderstanding. People sometimes interpret words differently because of varying experience, knowledge, vocabulary, culture, background, and attitudes. A good speaker uses tone of voice, facial expressions, and mannerisms to help make the message clear to the listener.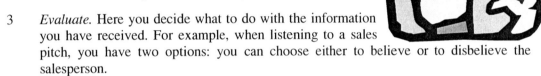

3   *Evaluate*. Here you decide what to do with the information you have received. For example, when listening to a sales pitch, you have two options: you can choose either to believe or to disbelieve the salesperson.

4   *Respond*. This is a verbal or visual response that lets the speaker know that you have got the message and what your reaction is.

Becoming a better listener

To communicate better with your customers, concentrate on listening more effectively. The following pointers will help.

Confirm your understanding   Imagine you are a tape recorder. Try to play back the speaker's words accurately. Restating the speaker's concepts will help you to concentrate, and you will indicate to the speaker that you understand correctly:

> "As I understand it, the problem is ..." *or* "Do you mean...?"

You are reassuring the speaker that you are both talking about the same thing.

Clarify by asking questions   If there is something you don't understand, ASK.

Don't jump to conclusions   Many people tune a speaker out when they think they have the gist of the conversation or know what he or she is going to say next. However, maybe the speaker is not following the same train of thought as you, or is not planning to make the point you think he or she is. If you don't listen, you may miss the real point the speaker is trying to get across.

Read the speaker's body language People don't always say what they mean, but their body language is usually an accurate indication of their meaning. A lot of clues to meaning come from the speaker's tone of voice, their facial expressions and gestures. For example, your boss may want to advise you that you dress rather too scruffily. S/he may use light-hearted words (so as not to appear too heavy-handed), but their body language might indicate that you shouldn't be misled into thinking that they are not therefore serious about the message.

Be aware of your own body language Make eye contact – it helps you to focus on the message, not the environment and will draw the speaker out to give information. Don't stare though! Don't fiddle or fold your arms as this forms a barrier.

Don't let yourself be distracted Don't be distracted by the environment or the speaker's appearance, accent or mannerisms.

Keep an open mind Don't just listen for statements that back up your own opinions and support your beliefs, or for certain parts that interest you. The point of listening, after all, is to gain new information.

Provide feedback Encouraging, non-committal statements will keep a speaker comfortable. The speaker will appreciate your interest and feel that you are really listening.

"I see" *or* "Mmm, carry on."

Go in with a positive attitude To get the most out of a meeting, speech, or conversation, say to yourself, "What can I learn from this to make me more valuable in my industry and to my company?"

Exercise 11

Imagine you work in a DIY shop and a customer said to you "I like your range of paints for house interiors, but of course wallpaper is what everyone seems to be using these days". Make brief notes about the four stages of the listening process after hearing this comment:

1   Hearing ....

2   Interpretation ....

3   Evaluation..

4   Response..

What extra information would you like to find out from the customer before taking any action?

....

....

....

....

Ineffective listening - What *not* to do

When it comes to listening, many of us are guilty of at least some bad habits. For example:

- Instead of listening while someone is talking, do you think about what you're going to say next?

- Are you easily distracted by the speaker's mannerisms or what is going on around you?

- Do you frequently interrupt people before they have finished talking?

- Do you drift off into daydreams because you are sure you know what the speaker is going to say?

All of these habits can hinder our listening ability. Contrary to popular notion, listening is not a passive activity. It requires full concentration and active involvement and is, in fact, hard work.

Exercise 12

Check your listening skills by reading through these comments from customers, then indicate whether you think the statements which follow are true or false.

1   Client to Training Centre administrator: "I love your training courses. The last course I attended was a 'beginners' course, but I learnt loads."

	True	False
The client thought the previous course was too easy.	☐	☐
The client thought the previous course was valuable.	☐	☐
The client would like to book onto another course.	☐	☐

2   Customer to sales department: "I'd like to meet up with one of your account managers when they visit my area. I have a few questions about your products that I would like to ask."

	True	False
Your products probably aren't right for this customer.	☐	☐
The customer isn't particularly impressed with your products.	☐	☐
The customer has already decided to buy some of your products.	☐	☐

3   Customer to personal fitness trainer. "I need to lose some weight but I don't have much time to go the gym."

	True	False
The customer would be interested to hear about appropriate fitness routines but doesn't have a lot of spare time.	☐	☐
The customer is going to cancel her gym membership.	☐	☐
The customer doesn't enjoy going to the gym.	☐	☐

Being an Active Listener

Active listening is a technique for listening and responding that focuses attention on the speaker.

The listener concentrates fully on what the speaker is saying, and then repeats, in the listener's own words, what he or she thinks the speaker has said.

The purpose of this is to ensure that both the speaker and listener know that the speaker has been understood. The listener does not have to *agree* with what is being said, but must make it clear what he or she *understands* is being said.

Active listening has several benefits.

- It forces you to listen attentively to the speaker. If you know you will have to repeat something in your own words, you tend to concentrate harder.

- It avoids misunderstandings, as you have to confirm that you really do understand what the speaker has said.

- It tends to encourage the speaker to say more.

Active listening will help you in two major ways when you are dealing with customers.

1   It will help you to **double-check** that you have understood the customer correctly.

2   It will enable you to get **feedback** from the customer to confirm that you have understood their needs correctly.

Active listening techniques

Active listening can include any, or all, of the following techniques:

- Encouraging,

- Rephrasing,

- Summarising.

Encouraging

You might encourage the speaker by using eye contact, positive body language, and saying things like "I see…", "Uh huh", or "That's interesting". You are not agreeing or disagreeing, but are *showing your interest* and encouraging the other person to keep talking.

Rephrasing

Rephrasing (or 'paraphrasing') means repeating the same thing back to the speaker, but using *different words*. This is to show your understanding of the facts, or the argument. You might have got it wrong, in which case this is an opportunity for the speaker to correct you.

Example of rephrasing

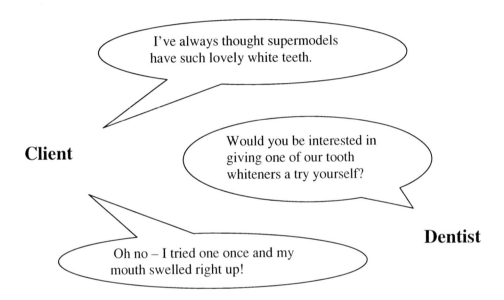

Here the dentist rephrases the client's comment and discovers that the client was just making a comment rather than a request. The **feedback** from the client is that she isn't interested in trying tooth whiteners as she seems to be allergic.

Summarising

You summarise what a speaker has said by briefly *pulling all the important facts* together, when he or she has finished speaking.

You might say "These seem to be the main points you have made…", or "So, to summarise what you want me do…", or:

"Do you mean that speed and accuracy are the key factors here?"

Exercise 13

Read through the following talk that your manager has with you.

Your Manager: I'd like to hold a *Customer Focus Group* meeting next month. I think we should invite the four biggest spending customers, and two customers that we have recently lost. Can you check the sales records. We can fit in two more – I'd like to choose two who have sent in suggestions by email, you will know who is appropriate. I'll need to draft an agenda by the end of the week and for that I need a summary of comments from our suggestion boxes and from the website feedback form. Can you get me all the information by Wednesday lunchtime, please.

Summarise the key information that you need to take away to make sure you give your manager what s/he needs.

....

....

....

....

Exercise 14

Rephrase the following comments from customers to check that you understand correctly what the customer means.

"That wallpaper is mind-blowing!"

....

....

"This computer system has a lot of extra accessories in the price."

....

....

"I see that your car cleaning service takes a whole hour."

....

....

Asking Questions

At work, we often need to gain additional knowledge and information in order to satisfy a particular request from a customer or to further a project.

Sometimes a customer won't be able to put over their point of view, request, question, complaint, etc, adequately. It is then up to you to find out the information by questioning the customer to draw out the information you need to know.

When doing this you will need to use *effective questioning skills* in order to obtain the information that you require.

Closed questions

Some questions are designed to gain a brief short answer, often Yes or No, and are used to establish something definite. They are called 'closed questions' and tend to begin with Can, Did, Do, Have, Is, Will and Would. Closed questions are useful in order to elicit information that is uncontroversial and doesn't need much discussion.

For example,

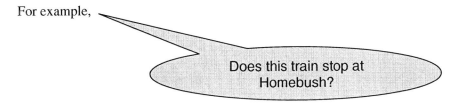

Does this train stop at Homebush?

However, closed questions are not helpful when you want your listener to open up and offer information. Have a look at the closed questions below.

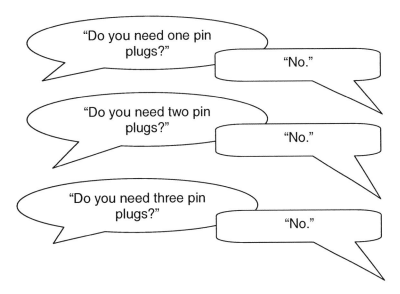

"Do you need one pin plugs?"

"No."

"Do you need two pin plugs?"

"No."

"Do you need three pin plugs?"

"No."

If the client needs 24 pin plugs, this conversation could go on for a very long time!

Open questions

Open questions, however, leave the topic "open" for a longer answer and further discussion, giving the speaker a chance to talk freely. This is a better kind of question to ask when trying to elicit information from a customer, eg rather than continuing the above line of questioning by asking:

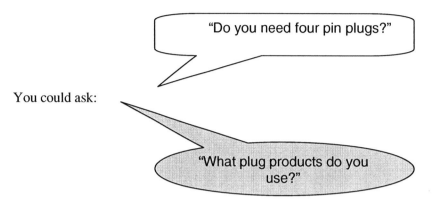

"Do you need four pin plugs?"

You could ask:

"What plug products do you use?"

Open questions tend to start with How, What, When, Where, Who, Why.

Exercise 15

For each of the following closed questions, write down an *open* question that will encourage the customer to talk to you.

Is everything alright with your meal?

....

Would you like me to show you our full range of pens?

....

Shall I wrap that for you?

....

Leading questions

When questioning a customer you should avoid questions that expect a particular answer and might therefore lead the person into answering untruthfully or unthinkingly. For example, if you were asked:

> "You paid back all the money that you owed your mother, didn't you?"

…. you might be too embarrassed to admit that you hadn't yet repaid the debt.

Similarly,

> "We've lost the petty cash box but you weren't in the office at all yesterday, were you?"

Here the speaker obviously doesn't think you were in the office yesterday, so you may agree with him/her without really thinking about the question. If you thought harder you might remember nipping into the office at lunchtime and seeing a stranger near the office manager's desk.

Double questions

Beware of "double questions" that actually require a complex answer to more than one clear point.

> "Is it the case that our marketing campaign hasn't been very successful, or are all our competitors finding the market to be very slow?"

The listener would find this a confusing question to answer as there are two different issues rolled into one question. Whether the campaign was unsuccessful or whether competitors are finding the market to be very slow are separate matters.

Exercise 16

Suggest an open question that the following people might ask to find out what their customers want.

1   An estate agent

....

....

2   A painter and decorator

....

....

3   A training course presenter

....

....

4   A fitness instructor

....

....

5   A wedding caterer

....

....

Notes

Who Should Help Customers?

When delivering a service to customers, first you need to decide whether you can help the customer *yourself*.

However,

- *The customer may request something that is outside your area of **knowledge**.*

  For example, a customer may ask about his unpaid account or about job opportunities for his daughter. If you don't know anything about these matters, then you will need to refer the customer to another, more appropriate, department, which has the *knowledge* required to deal with the enquiry. These queries may be better handled by the accounts department and by the human resources department.

- *The customer may request something that is outside your **authority**.*

  For example, a customer may need a refund or to return goods, which you do not have the authority to authorise. In these instances you will need to refer the customer to your manager or another person who has the *authority* to respond to the enquiry.

If you can help, then do so, but you must pass the customer on if you can't help or are unsure.

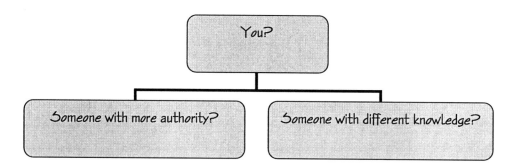

Helping Customers Yourself

➢ Be prompt – customers come first, so attend to their enquiry before your other tasks.

➢ Be honest – can you help the customer? If not, admit it now rather than stringing the customer along, otherwise you may end up wasting their time.

➢ Do what you say you will do – if you promise to post information today, make sure it goes out today. If it cannot - for an unavoidable reason - then make sure that the customer is informed of the delay and when their request will be attended to.

➢ If a customer doesn't need your help at the moment, remain available to them so that if they change their mind they know where you are.

Referring Customers

If you cannot handle a particular request you should refer the customer to a different person for help. This is perfectly acceptable and is far preferable to trying to answer a query when you either don't know the answer or don't have the authority to do what you purport to do.

Don't be embarrassed to say that you are not able to handle a particular request. Most customers will be grateful that you are upfront with them rather than stringing them along and wasting their time. However, you must assist the customer by finding out who is the appropriate person for them to speak to and by ensuring that the customer is put into contact with that person in an appropriate way.

When should customers be referred?

You should refer customers when their enquiries are outside your:

- area of knowledge, or

- authority.

You should then refer the customer to a member of staff who has the relevant knowledge and/or authority. For example, a bank clerk would probably be able to answer enquiries such as:

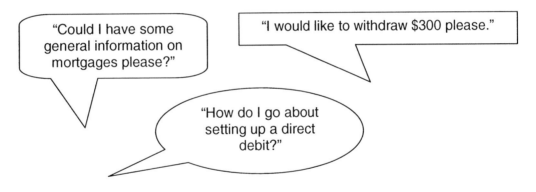

However, the same clerk would not be able to answer queries such as:

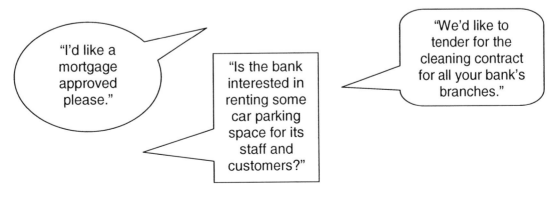

Who should customers be referred to?

You may need to refer customers to any of the following.

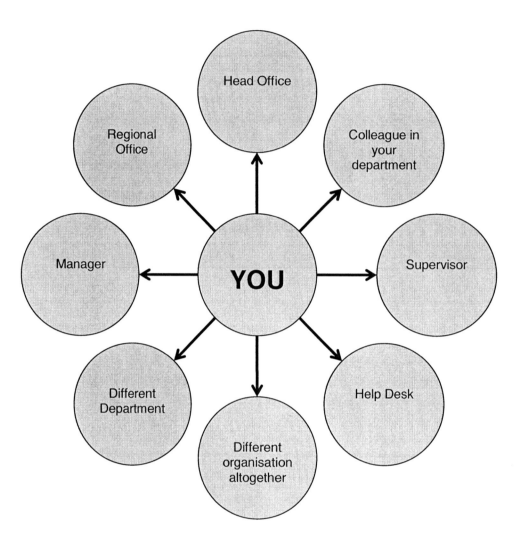

Examples

- **Head office** – customers who need a higher level of advice or assistance may need to be referred to head office. This might be the case if, for instance, they need information on the organisation itself, rather than just products or services.

- **Regional office** – customers who are geographically nearer to another of your offices or departments, may best be referred to that branch rather than being dealt with by your office.

- **A colleague in the same department as you** – customers may need to be dealt with by a colleague who has dealt with the customer previously and who knows the background to their account and/or query.

- **Your manager or supervisor** – a customer who needs advice which it is beyond your authority to give will need to be referred to your supervisor. Customers who complain about a colleague who does not report to you, should usually be referred to a manager.

- **Someone in a different department or team** – customers with a query about an invoice may need to be referred to the accounting department or a customer who wants marketing information may best be referred to the marketing team.

- **Help Desk** – customers with technical questions or who need hands-on help may be referred to a Help Desk or telephone helpline or hotline.

- **Different organisation altogether** - eg a medical centre receptionist may recommend a caller with an emergency goes to the local hospital or dials 000.

Alternatively, your organisation might state that certain people always deal with certain problems. So, for example,

- In a charity, all enquiries about accounts payable (ie bills that the charity has to pay) might have to be referred to the Accounts Payable Clerk.

- In a manufacturing company, all enquiries about orders might have to go to Customer Services.

- In a veterinary clinic, all enquiries about stray animals may have to go to the local SPCA office.

- In a school, all enquiries about punishment of pupils may have to go to the Board of Governors.

In these cases, all enquiries in these fields would be referred to the person or department which has been *nominated* as the appropriate one.

Exercise 17

1   Would a motor insurance clerk answer the following queries him/herself or would s/he refer the customer to someone else (and if so who).

"Can you give me a quote for insuring my laptop computer?" ....

"I think your motor insurance quote is far too high, can you reduce it?" ....

"I'd like to rent a car for the holiday period." ....

2   Would an assistant librarian answer the following questions him/herself or would s/he refer the customer to someone else (and if so who).

"Do you have a dictionary in stock?" ....

"Can I work part-time here over the Christmas break?" ....

"How much money did the library make over the past year?" ....

How to refer customers

- Keep the customer informed as to what you are doing and why you are doing it.

- Contact the new staff member yourself – don't point the customer towards the staff member and make them find him or her.

- Don't make the customer repeat their instructions or request – pass the information on yourself to the new staff member.

- Make sure that the new staff member follows up the enquiry and deals with it – otherwise it will reflect badly on you.

Exercise 18

If you are currently in a job, make a note here of people to whom you might often have to refer customers. Note their name, title, area of responsibility or knowledge and where to find them (office, branch, phone number etc). This will save you time when customers enquire.

....

....

....

....

Customers who may not want to be referred

If a previous member of staff has already passed a customer on to **you**, the customer may be reluctant to be transferred to another member of staff if you decide that you cannot assist the customer either.

It is very annoying to be passed from person to person as you will know if you have ever had this happen to you. In this situation, give the customer the option of you tracking down the correct person and having them call the customer back. If you do this, you should:

(a) Give the customer your own name and phone number so that they still have a contact to come back to, and

(b) Ensure that the other staff member does call the customer back. If they are not available straightaway then call the customer back yourself to keep them up-to-date with what is happening.

Good Customer Relations

When you meet customers, you are responsible for ensuring that they receive a good first impression of your company, so you must be courteous, smart, professional, friendly and attentive at all times. You must make customers feel welcome, important and individual. This is called 'establishing a rapport' or 'establishing good customer relations'. The following factors will assist you in establishing a good rapport with customers.

Be prompt

A customer must never be kept waiting unnecessarily, and must never feel ignored. If you are dealing with another customer you should make eye contact with the next customer and smile to acknowledge their presence. If you are on the phone, make eye contact, smile, and bring the phone conversation to a close as quickly as possible. Never continue talking with another staff member or friend while a customer is waiting.

Your manner and attitude

Make the customer enjoy dealing with you! Your attitude will be conveyed in many different ways. It is important that:

- Your manner is helpful and courteous.

- Your tone is friendly because your voice mirrors your personality and feeling and indicates your mood.

- You put a smile in your voice and are enthusiastic.

Your voice

- Your speech should be clear and concise.

- Keep monotony out of your voice. Have peaks and valleys for interesting contrast. This helps to hold attention. Keep the less important words in the valleys.

- Any speech habit that calls attention to itself and detracts from the message is undesirable.

Use the customer's name

You should try to develop a good memory, identifying regular callers. Politely ask for the customer's name and then make sure you use it.

If it is your organisation's policy to address customers using their *first* name, you should check that it is appropriate for you to address the customer that way before becoming too familiar. For example, you might say, "Is it alright if I call you Percy?"

If a customer's origin and culture are unfamiliar to you, and you find their name tricky to spell or pronounce, you should repeat it back to the customer to ensure that you are pronouncing and/or spelling it correctly.

Special tips when dealing with customers *on the telephone*

Remember that when dealing with customers over the telephone, the caller relies on the sound of your voice and the quality of your response to make a decision about how good your company is. Don't fall into the trap of thinking that because the telephone is impersonal you can give bad service and get away with it!

Workers who may use the telephone a lot at work include

- Call centre workers,

- Helpline support staff,

- Researchers,

- Lawyers,

- Taxi company managers, etc.

Good telephone answering technique

- Answer the telephone promptly - always before the third ring. Leaving a phone to ring will irritate your co-workers and will give the caller the impression that his/her call is not important to your company. It also may be essential to answer promptly if the telephone is hooked up to an answer phone, otherwise the call might be diverted.

- Greet the caller. Say "Good Morning" or "Good Afternoon" first, because often the first words you say are not heard clearly.

- State the name of your company or your department clearly.

- State your name.

- Offer to help, for example "How may I help you?"

- Sound friendly and interested but professional.

- Keep a smile in your voice.

Exercise 19

Write down how you would respond in the following situations.

1   A diner at your restaurant gives you her credit card to pay the bill. The name on the card is Mrs Jennie Wilson. What do you say to the diner when you return her credit card?

....

....

2   You are on the phone to a friend. He is in the middle of telling you a very interesting piece of gossip when a customer walks in. What do you do?

....

....

Exercise 20

How do you think the customer in the following scenario would rate each of the following comments by the waitress in terms of good customer relations. Pick a number between 1 and 5 where 1 is 'Very good' and 5 is 'Very poor'.

Scenario: Margery Collins has been going to the same café for breakfast most Saturdays ever since she moved to the district – about three months ago. She likes the chatty atmosphere and enjoys taking time over coffee there.

Waitress's comments:

"Morning. I'll be back in a minute for your order."	1	2	3	4	5
"We stop serving breakfast at 10.30 sharp, so you'll need to order quickly."	1	2	3	4	5
"Hello Margery, it's a lovely day, isn't it? What would you like to eat today?"	1	2	3	4	5
"Good morning Margery. We've just had some new customers in, so I'll serve you last if you don't mind."	1	2	3	4	5

What Products and Services Can You Offer to Your Customers?

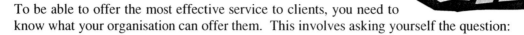

To be able to offer the most effective service to clients, you need to know what your organisation can offer them. This involves asking yourself the question:

What does my organisation provide?

By way of example, here are some situations where a customer may be confused, and the questions the customer might ask. If you worked for these organisations, you would have to know enough about the services you offer to be able to answer these questions accurately.

<table>
<tr><td>

A car rental firm

"Does this rental firm only rent out cars, or does it rent motor homes too? Does the rental price include the insurance cost? Is there a discount on the price if I rent the vehicle out for a long period? Can I drop the vehicle off at a different location to where I picked it up?"

</td><td>

A gymnasium

"Do I need to join this gym for a fixed period of time, or can I just pay whenever I visit? Is there a special rate for people who visit during the day rather than at peak times, such as the evenings? Are there special fitness classes laid on, and if so, are they included in the joining fee?"

</td></tr>
<tr><td>

A bookshop

"Is there a loyalty card scheme at this bookshop? If I start reading a book and don't like it, can I exchange it? Also if I buy a book for my friend's birthday and she already has it, can she return it? Maybe it would be better to get a gift voucher for her, do you do those? If so, how long are they valid for?"

</td><td>

A Computer Training School

"I have already worked on a computer for a couple of months; do I qualify as 'beginner' or 'intermediate'? Can I bring in my own examples of tasks that I have to do at work to go through, or do you have a strict syllabus that you stick to? If I find the course difficult, do you provide printouts that I can take home and read through?"

</td></tr>
</table>

Exercise 21

Choose one of the situations above and list three pieces of information that you would need to find out in order to answer some of the customer's questions.

Situation chosen: ....

....

....

....

Gathering information

To find out what your organisation offers, you need to *talk*, *listen* and *read*.

TALK to your supervisor, your manager and your colleagues. Ask questions if there is anything you don't understand. Don't be embarrassed even if it seems quite a basic or silly question. You will feel sillier later on if a customer asks you the same question and you can't answer it!

LISTEN to what is said to you. You may need to take notes to ensure that you remember as much information as possible, particularly at the start of a new job when you can suffer from "information overload". Information overload is when we get that feeling that our head will explode if we try and take in any more information!

READ as much material as you can get your hands on regarding your job and the wider organisation. In particular, you should make sure that you are familiar with:

➤ Product catalogues

➤ Service manuals

➤ Guidelines and procedures documents

➤ The organisational chart

Remember you must know your organisation's products and services inside out, so you can offer appropriate advice and guidance.

Exercise 22

What services or products does your organisation (or ideal organisation) provide? List three of them here.

....

....

....

Exercise 23

Write down three questions that a customer might ask you about the services or products offered by your organisation (or ideal organisation). Make sure you know the correct answers!

....

....

....

Helping Customers Choose the Right Service or Product

Once you know what your organisation provides, you are armed with the information to help the customer.

Some transactions that you have with customers will be relatively straightforward.

A customer may, for instance, ask you a simple question to which you know the answer.

> Do these electrical appliances come with a warranty?

> Yes, all appliances come with a three-year warranty. You just need to keep hold of your receipt.

However, in some situations, a customer may need assistance in deciding which is the best service for them. By helping them choose well, you can maximise the chance that the customer will come away from their dealings with you happy and satisfied.

The worst case scenario is for customers to come away from you disappointed. It is a fact that few customers complain to organisations about the service they have received. However, you can bet your bottom dollar that they will complain to *someone*. If it isn't you, it will be their family, friends and colleagues – all of whom are potential customers of yours and who won't form a good opinion of you.

Providing the RIGHT service to customers, has two steps to it.

1   Involve the customer - find out what *they* want from the product or service,

2   Help the customer to make the final choice.

Involve the customer

Use appropriate body language

Use appropriate body language, as discussed earlier in this book, to show the customer that you are interested in them and want to assist them.

Imagine you were interested in buying an outfit for a big party at the weekend and you were greeted by the shop assistant on the right.

It is likely that this young lady would take away any initial enthusiasm you felt and put a damper on your keenness to buy anything in her particular shop. It's likely that you would try elsewhere.

However, what if this shop assistant greeted you ….

Being met by someone smiling and interested in helping you makes all the difference. It is much more likely that you would enjoy being served by this lady, and would be interested to hear her views on what the shop stocks and what accessories might be appropriate to complement what you choose.

Use your listening and questioning skills

Talk to the customer to find out what it is that they actually want, and what their views are. If you listen carefully, you may begin to realise that what the client *thinks* they want wouldn't be appropriate for the job they have in mind.

Example 1: Garden Centre

Lisa goes to a garden centre. She likes the look of the new range of lawnmowers that has just arrived and is examining them intently. Claude, the assistant, says hello. He has lots of knowledge about the lawnmowers and can't wait to tell Lisa about their engine power, non-tip security and electrical cut-out safety features. He goes on at some length and Lisa can't get a word in edgeways. However, she is impressed by Claude's knowledge so she feels sure that he will select her a good machine, which he does.

After thanking Claude profusely, Lisa gets to the checkout and casually mentions to the checkout assistant that she is looking forward to trimming the edges of her lawn with her fantastic new machine. The checkout assistant looks concerned and tells her that the model she has been given doesn't have that facility. He calls Claude over and Lisa is taken back to the lawn section to look at the lawn edge cutters instead.

What did Claude do wrong?

Claude didn't ask Lisa what she actually wanted to use the gardening item for. Lisa mistakenly thought that she needed a lawnmower, but in actual fact she needed a lawn edger. Because Lisa didn't get a chance to talk about what she wanted, Claude assumed wrongly that she had already decided on buying a lawnmower and he proceeded to tell her all about them.

When Lisa did get a chance to talk to someone, luckily the checkout assistant was listening and was able to correct her!

When talking to customers, try to find out as much *general* information about them as well as *specific* information about what they want from you. This will trigger ideas that neither of you might otherwise have come up with.

Example 2: Computer shop

Simon is a computer salesman. He noticed that other computer salespeople asked their customers very direct questions, such as "Do you want a powerful computer? Do you need a printer? Do you want a scanner?"

Simon realised that customers probably didn't know the different models of computer very well. They also wouldn't necessarily know the full range of uses for all the different accessories they could buy. Therefore, Simon realised that customers might not have all the information they needed in order to be able to answer these questions properly.

So Simon started asking more general, open questions like "How often are the children going to be doing their homework on the computer?" "Do you have to deal with a lot of large documents for your work?" "Are you interested in setting up a home office from where you can link to your network at work?" "How often do your friends and family send you digital photos for you to look at on screen?" "Would you like to be able to print those photos out?"

By asking more about what the customers would <u>do</u> with their computer, Simon found he got a much clearer and more comprehensive picture of how customers would **use** their computer and what **features** they would find useful.

In this way he was able to suggest and explain all the different computer accessories and features that customers might benefit from.

Remember first and foremost that the service or product that you provide must fit the purpose for which the customer wants it.

Making the final choice

When you and the customer have thoroughly explored all the options, you may have narrowed the selection of products or services down to two or three options, all of which fit the **purpose** for which the customer needs the product or service.

You could then discuss the following factors to assist the customer to make the final decision.

Price – How does the price of this product/service compare with the price for similar products/services. If there is a range of products/services at different prices, why is each one priced as it is?

Features – What features does this product/service have that cheaper similar products/services *don't* have? What features doesn't it have that more expensive similar products/services *do* have?

Maintenance – Will the product need servicing in the future? Will it have to be sent away to the manufacturer's workshop? Does the product come with a warranty?

Flexibility – Can the product be used for anything other than what the customer needs it for – for example can a digital camera also be used as a web cam? Is it more or less versatile than similar products?

Upgrading – Is it a new product with all the latest features, or is it about to become an 'old generation' product line? Will the product become obsolete or could it be upgraded?

Shelf life – Is the product likely to be quickly superseded by new developments?

Accessories – Can the customer add on other products to this one to make it more functional?

Your approach

Think of services and products that your organisation provides as special. If *you* think well of the services you can offer, you are more likely to be able to communicate that to your customers.

When discussing products and services, ensure that you focus on the positive rather than the negative. For example, if the customer wishes to compare a product or service with one offered by a competitor, concentrate on what is good about your product or service, rather than what you think is wrong with the competing product or service.

Exercise 24

Imagine that you are a travel agent and your customer is trying to decide whether to have a weekend break in Australia or whether to fly to Fiji for a week's holiday. Write down three questions that you could ask about the customer's expectations that would help the customer decide which was the most appropriate holiday to take.

....

....

....

Delivering the Service

Your organisation's requirements

In the same way that most workplaces have a dress code (whether official or unofficial) many workplaces will have requirements about certain service procedures.

Whether it is the colour of the paper you should use when writing letters, the form of greeting you give to customers when talking to them on the phone, or the way you should handle complaints, the chances are your organisation will have rules which you should follow.

These rules or requirements may cover such matters as:

- How quickly the phone is to be answered

- Recommended form of words to use when the phone is answered

- Form of greeting when a customer arrives at reception

- Person to whom all customer complaints should be referred

- Way to record orders and how to ensure they are satisfied

- When to exchange goods rather than refund purchase price

- What form of payment to allow

- When to give a discount.

Workplaces have these rules to ensure that all customers are treated in an appropriate, consistent and fair way, regardless of who they deal with in the organisation. The rules give employees a framework so that they know what is expected of them – by the organisation and by customers.

> For instance,
>
> The rule regarding personal presentation may be "All sales representatives must wear a suit and tie".
>
> The rule regarding greeting customers on the phone might be "All receptionists must say Good Morning or Afternoon, give the organisation's name, their own name and say 'How may I help you?'"

Example

Jennie is a travel agent. The travel agency specialises in expensive cruises, weddings-on-the-beach, honeymoons and 'once-in-a-lifetime' holiday breaks. The agency's customers spend a lot of money on very special holidays and so the travel agency has rules on:

- the personal presentation of the travel agents – smart suits to be worn,

- the style of furniture in the office – leather sofas and mahogany desks,

- the way that customers are addressed - as Sir and Madam,

- how customers are greeted - they are always offered a cup of tea or coffee, and

- the way that their enquiries are discussed - customers sit in comfy sofas, and are given a slide show of hotels and resorts from the region they are interested in. They are also given colour brochures to take away and offered the chance to meet with satisfied customers who have already taken their holiday.

Where to find information on your organisation's requirements

Requirements as to how you deal with customers could be contained in any of the following:

- Guidelines

- Quality assurance manual

- Job description

- Employment contract

- Workplace manual

- Workplace Guide

- Recommended Procedures Guide

- Pricing and discount policy documentation

- Replacement and refund policy and procedures

- Payment and delivery options documentation

- Health and safety procedures

- Anti-discrimination policy

- Your organisation's intranet.

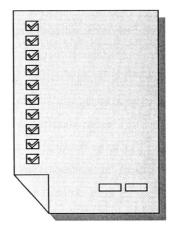

If you have a job, ask your supervisor to help you find the requirements if there are any and bear them in mind when you are reading the next sections of this Workbook.

On the next two pages are some requests that customers will make that crop up in a range of businesses and environments, together with information you must have before you can respond.

Making referrals to other colleagues or departments

If you are unable to assist a customer, you will need to refer them to a colleague, a different department or a different branch of your organisation. Ensure that you tell the customer whom you are going to refer them to and why. Make sure that the customer has your contact number and that of the person to whom you are referring them in case of any problems.

Ensure that the person you are referring the customer to is the correct person and, if circumstances permit, explain the circumstances to your colleague beforehand so that they know what the nature of the enquiry will be.

For example, you may need to refer customers who have:

- problems with accounts to accounts payable or receivable

- problems with ordering to the sales department

- complaints about service to your manager

- foreign enquiries to your international office or head office.

Giving information on returning your organisation's products and services

You must know company policy – have you read the replacement and refund policy document?

You must know the correct procedure.

You must know if you have the authority to accept returned goods and, if you don't, who to refer customers to.

Giving general information about the company

To be helpful to customers, you must have a sound knowledge of the company, its structure, its people and its products.

You must be aware of the company's mission statement.

You must know who's who in the company, and who are the key people who can help if the customer asks a question about certain matters, eg who deals with ordering, delivery problems, arranging sales visits, etc.

You should keep up-to-date phone extension lists, lists of branches and offices, head office details, documents on company structure and an organisational chart near to hand.

Giving advice or general information

You may need to give out general information, eg directions to your building or office. For these kinds of request, you should keep to hand a local map, list of bus routes, train times, an office plan, etc. In addition, is your organisation often mistaken for another? If appropriate, you could keep details of the other company on hand so that you can helpfully redirect customers (be wary of directing customers to your competitors!).

Clarifying or resolving problems or complaints

You should check that you know company policy on the matter and check that it is within your area of authority. Question the customer to ensure you get all the details. Ask the customer what he/she expects - it could be that all they want is for their complaint to be recorded. Then tell the customer what you intend to do. Be as prompt as possible in getting back to the customer with your decision. If you need more time to investigate the complaint then explain this to the customer. If the company is not at fault, make sure you explain this.

Giving information on purchasing your organisation's products and services

You must know company policy on pricing and discounting.

You must know the correct procedures for how to purchase.

You must know who is the correct person or department to assist the customer (if not you).

Giving specific information about your products or services

You must know all the company's products or services.

You must know how the products or services are sold.

You must know what products or services are currently being advertised (ie are any on special offer, are any new ones being introduced?).

Have easy access to order forms, price lists, catalogues, internet, intranet, etc.

Making appointments

To arrange appointments, you will need to have your diary in front of you. This could be a paper diary or an electronic one.

If you need to make appointments for other people or for a group of people, it is often useful if diaries are electronic and on a computer network to which you have access – you can then check availability of all the relevant people at the same time without having to contact them all individually.

Helpful resources

When dealing with customers, you need to be able to react promptly and efficiently. You may find the following equipment and reference materials useful, though not all of these items will apply to all organisations or all employees. Think about what it would be useful to have access to and make a note - then ensure that you have easy access to it at all times.

Equipment	Reference materials
<ul><li>Pen</li><li>Paper</li><li>Calculator</li><li>Your diary</li><li>Telephone</li><li>Email system</li><li>Voice mail</li></ul>	<ul><li>Phone list – internal extensions and useful external numbers.</li><li>An up-to-date price list.</li><li>A list of guidelines for internal procedures.</li><li>Company catalogues and literature.</li><li>Organisational chart.</li><li>Company details, including phone number, box number, fax, email address, web site, etc.</li><li>Customer database - extract information about regular customers so you can be more knowledgeable when speaking to them.</li><li>Any other databases that would help you answer questions.</li><li>Account information - if you have to phone customers back, would it help to know their account details?</li><li>Is there an internet or intranet of company information? Can you offer access to that to customers? They could then have up-to-date information at their fingertips.</li></ul>

What services will customers need?

Customers will have all sorts of needs that they need your help with.

- The sales manager could ask you to write a report on your department's performance, or

- A manufacturer could order 40 hub caps for urgent delivery through your website, or

- A diner could request that you cater for 100 people at his/her daughter's wedding, or

- A user could ring your telephone helpline to ask for technical support in installing your products.

You never know what a customer is going to request – it depends on the business you are in. Customers might want **advice, support, information, instructions** or many other things. Being able to recognise the kind of help that customers want will assist you in delivering the appropriate service to them.

Exercise 26

Listed below are seven requests that a customer may make. Match up the customers with the response they need by writing the letter of the appropriate response next to the statement.

REQUEST	RESPONSE
( ) "I need a computer for my daughter to do her homework on, but I know nothing about them!"	(a) Referral to another department or colleague
( ) "Can you help me install this spa pool that I bought from you last week?"	(b) Advice on ordering or registration procedures
( ) "Your lawn mowing service has left huge mud patches in my front garden!"	(c) Information about products or services
( ) "I'd like to sign up with the gym, please."	(d) Information about the company
( ) "I need to talk to someone about mortgages – who shall I come and see and when?"	(e) Practical assistance
( ) "I have always spoken to Trudie previously, perhaps it would be best if I talk to her again?"	(f) Arrange an appointment
( ) "Does your company have a New Zealand operation?"	(g) Resolve or clarify a problem

---

Assisting customers correctly

Scenario: A customer telephones an internet email helpline with a query.

Billy: Good morning, Inter-Access helpline, this is Billy speaking. How may I help you?

Millicent: This is Millicent Parks. My internet user name is Millicent99, and my password is 47393. My husband would like to join your service and have his own email address. How do I go about organising that?

Billy: Right, I don't handle charging queries. I'll need to put you through to our accounts department.

Millicent: It's not a charging query, I just want to set up an email account for my husband.

Billy: Right, can you give me your user name and password please?

Millicent: Yes, my user name is Millicent99, and my password is 47393.

Billy: Okay, to set up your husband's email account we'll need your husband's details. I'm new here so I'm not sure what we need. I'm putting you on hold.

Billy's manager: Yes, what is it now Billy?

Millicent: Oh, Billy must have put me through. My name is Millicent. Can you help me set up an account for my husband?

Billy has made several mistakes in dealing with the customer. Can you name two?

1 ....

2 ....

Billy made the following mistakes.

1   Billy didn't listen properly to what Millicent's request was and Millicent had to explain twice. Billy also did not listen to the information that Millicent gave him. Millicent had to repeat her user name and password details. **SOLUTION**: Use your listening skills.

2   Billy didn't have enough information to be able to help Millicent with what appears to be a relatively straightforward question. **SOLUTION**: Read all available materials on workplace procedures.

3   Billy did not explain to Millicent that he was putting her on hold or that he was transferring her to someone (his manager) who might be better able to assist her. **SOLUTION**: Use your interpersonal skills to treat people appropriately and politely.

4   Finally, Billy did not speak to his manager first and explain Millicent's request in order to ensure that his manager could help her. He also didn't tell the manager that he was putting him through to Millicent and therefore the manager's greeting to Millicent was inappropriate and rather rude. **SOLUTION**: Check who customers should be referred to and check workplace guidelines on appropriate telephone etiquette.

Billy's lack of attention and discernment complicated the situation and resulted in Millicent receiving a poor service.

Scenario

The salesman in the examples below does not know how to help the customer. His responses leave rather a lot to be desired. Think about what is wrong with his answers before looking at the comments underneath.

1   "I don't understand that product. I'll find my manager and you can explain it all again."

2   "I'll see what I can do for you but I don't know when I'll be able to get back to you."

3   "We don't provide that service. I don't know why – it seems like we should. Tell you what, I'll find someone to do it today."

4   "Oh, you need the Brisbane office. Not us. Goodbye."

The salesman's responses were unacceptable because:

Response 1:   The salesman shouldn't have made the customer explain the problem for a second time.

Response 2:   The salesman should always give a timeframe in which he will get back to a customer. Even if he may not have been able to address the request, he should have given a date or time by which he would give the customer an update.

Response 3:   The salesman shouldn't have promised what he didn't know he could deliver. In this instance there may be a very good reason why his company does not offer the service that the customer wants. By promising the customer that he will sort it out, he is deterring the customer from getting satisfaction elsewhere which may put the customer off schedule and make the company look bad.

Response 4:   The salesman should have got the Brisbane details for the customer!

Deliver a service to customers   **53**

Write down how you would assist customers in the following situations.

Optician

A customer comes into the opticians and tells you that she has recently been getting bad headaches. She thinks she may be having difficulty seeing properly. She is worried that seeing the optician and buying spectacles may be out of her price range. How do you assist the customer?

....

....

....

Photo development kiosk

A customer tells you that they have four films to develop and they need to have two of the films developed in time to take the photos to a family reunion. They think that some family members might want to take copies away with them too. Some of the elderly family members have quite bad eyesight and find small photos difficult to see. How do you help this customer?

....

....

....

Clothing manufacturer

A shop manager who sells a lot of your ladies' clothing range in his shop says that the shop is branching out into men's clothing. He would like to know if your company can help on the marketing and distribution side, particularly if they open shops in other cities. How do you help this customer?

....

....

....

Beauty salon

A customer tells you that she would like to have a face lift and also to discuss training to be a beauty therapist. How do you help this customer?

....

....

....

Giving Information to Customers

When you are serving customers, you need the customer to listen to *you*. There are some key skills that you can develop which will retain people's interest while you speak to them and enable you to get your information or point of view across effectively.

Your voice and language

1   Develop a friendly, attractive voice. It is easy – especially if you feel shy – to speak in a monotone. However, the listener may well tune out if there are no "peaks" and "troughs" in your voice.

2   Speak clearly and loudly enough so that people can hear you and don't have to ask you to repeat yourself. Don't make a listener have to strain to hear you.

3   Watch your language. Your language will differ depending on who you are speaking to, eg your boss, a friend, a friend's mother, etc. We speak to all these people in different ways. In formal conversations, do not use slang words. Never swear at work.

What information to give

1   Establish what information is required. Give the key information required first, in case the customer is under time constraints.

2   Offer to discuss or explain further if required. If you don't give the customer the complete picture, make sure that they know they can come back to you at any time in the future for more information.

3   Issue brochures and/or information leaflets where applicable.

4   If you have been asked a question to which you do not know the answer, ask the customer to wait while you find someone who does know. Never guess as you will then either waffle or your body language will give you away!

Keeping listeners' attention

1   If you're speaking to a group, try directing your attention to various people in the room, one at a time. Make eye contact and speak directly to that person for a minute or so.

2   Ask questions. Whether they are rhetorical or demand some kind of response, questions keep the listener involved. When it comes to communicating, a two-way conversation is usually more effective than a lecture.

To finish

Ask the customer if your information/explanation has answered their query. Give them a chance to ask further questions until they are completely satisfied.

Exercise 28

Your colleague, Joan, tells you that recently a few customers have complained that she didn't give them the right information. She says that she did but the customer must have misunderstood or misheard. She asks for advice on improving her skills in giving information. You overhear her saying the following things to customers. What would you mention to her as areas for improvement.

Conversation 1

Joan: "You want to make an appointment to see Barbara? [Shouts to colleague: Hey Barbara, when are you free on Friday?] What on earth do you want to do that for, she's going to get the sack soon! No, only joking. Don't panic missus! Now, what was it you wanted again?"

Your comments:...

....

....

....

Conversation 2

Joan: "Okay, you want to know what products we stock? I'm not really sure but I'll have a guess. Well colours first - right, there's dark blue, mid-blue, light blue, dark green, mid-green, a kind of lawn green, fawn, beige, buff, brown and black. Did you get all that? All kinds of shapes and sizes too, I'll go through them all for you: not all of these will be relevant to you, but stop me if you get bored. Here we go - ..."

Your comments:...

....

....

....

Exercise 29

Answer the following questions on factors of good service.

1   It's important to know company policy before answering a customer's enquiry because:

       ....

       ....

2   Taking time to make sure a customer gets the right service is more important that dealing with them quickly and getting rid of them because:

       ....

       ....

Prioritising Customers' Requests

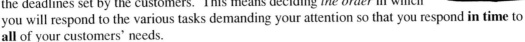

You will need to **prioritise** the needs of your various customers in order to ensure that you meet the deadlines imposed by your own organisation, and the deadlines set by the customers. This means deciding *the order* in which you will respond to the various tasks demanding your attention so that you respond **in time** to **all** of your customers' needs.

This involves *managing* your workload appropriately.

1   Identify what customers need from you and by when. Will you need to get information from someone else on a customer's behalf (this may delay you in responding)? Is a request urgent? When do your organisation's rules and procedures state that such tasks should be completed by?

2   Estimate how long a task might take. When do the customers want replies? What other tasks do you already have to do? Which have been waiting the longest to be actioned? Which have the most imminent deadlines?

Exercise 30

Prioritise the following tasks on a word processing operator's To Do List.

A: Type up Agenda for next month's board meeting for distribution by end of week.

B: Type up minutes from last month's board meeting for distribution before next board meeting.

C: Type notice for kitchen telling everyone to be a bit tidier.

D: Make a couple of small corrections in the letter Mrs Smyth needs to post today.

Your suggested order of priority: ....

Considerations

Urgency

Customers will need your services for specific reasons – sometimes they will be urgent, sometimes not. Sometimes they won't be urgent today, but may become so tomorrow!

The more detail you can get about timelines the better. Always remember to ask what the information is for, and when it is needed. It is up to you to ask. Don't wait to be told. If you do not know your deadline, you will either miss it, or end up in a last minute hurry with someone hounding you for the information.

A customer may give you a deadline by which he wants the product or service in place. Remember that although a customer may not tell you that something is urgent, s/he will still expect you to take action within a reasonable time.

Leanne works as an assistant at an advertising agency. One day a client, Bob of Pancake Bakery, tells her that he has a couple of contacts who are looking for a new advertising agency. Bob suggests Leanne puts together some information on the agency and the type of work that the agency does, for him to give to his contacts.

Leanne works very hard to put together a comprehensive information pack for the potential new clients.

When she rings Bob to let him know that the document is ready, Bob is uninterested. "Thanks, Leanne, but you are too late. They have already signed up with another agency!"

What could Leanne have done to avoid this wasted effort?

....

....

....

....

A chain of information

Customers may need your help so that they can solve a problem, pass the information on to their customers, achieve a goal, etc. If you don't provide your service when it is needed, then it is of no use – however well you may have done your job.

Remember, if you're relying on other people to provide you with information, or to make a decision, delays are to be expected and you should factor these into your estimate of when you will complete the task.

Be honest

If your service isn't provided in the timeframe in which you say it will be, you may well find that customers learn to distrust you and go elsewhere for help.

Let your customer know the date by which something will be done. If there is a delay for whatever reason, explain the reasons for a delay. This will bring the customer into the picture and reassure them that their request is progressing.

Aids to prioritising your time

1   *To Do* Lists. If all your tasks are written down in one place, you'll feel more in control of your job. A list helps you to compare each task and decide which to tackle first. A list held on your computer is easy to keep up-to-date.

2   Use your diary. By writing entries in your diary, you can see what needs to be done day-by-day and you are less likely to run out of time to complete the task.

3   Use a wall planner.

Standard turnaround times

Some workplaces have standard times in which a job should be completed.

Examples of turnaround times set by organisations

- Wilfred works in a bakery. He is expected to take no more than 90 minutes to turn around each batch of 50 loaves.

- Jenny makes patchwork quilts to order. Her standard turnaround time per quilt is three weeks.

- Fred installs fitted kitchens. His standard turnaround time for installation is two days.

Exercise 32

1   A customer at your hairdressing salon tells you they have to be in an important meeting in 45 minutes and need a hair cut. You know that hair cuts tend to take about an hour. What do you tell the customer?

....

....

2   Your manager tells you that she needs some documents photocopied for a meeting. She tells you just to fit the job in when you can. What do you say to your manager?

....

....

What Other Needs Do Customers Have?

Some customer needs will be less defined than simply needing information or needing to choose an appropriate product or service.

Imagine your organisation has a comments box. You find the following notes in the box one day. What can you tell about these customers from their comments?

Note 1

> When I need information I like to know that there is someone I can speak to. It's handy having the internet but sometimes I send an email and never get a reply - it's very frustrating.
>
> Now I always use the phone which is more time-consuming and sometimes I waste time being on hold, but at least I know I will talk to someone eventually.
>
> Bill

Note 2

> I need product to be delivered when I am told it will be. I prefer that you tell me it's out of stock and you don't know when it will be in than for you to guess and get it wrong - as you have in the past.
>
> I give my own customers a date based on your delivery date and I don't want to let them down. That reflects very badly on me.
>
> Hillary

Bill, who wrote Note 1, is commenting on communication with your organisation. Bill would like easy access to information and has learned not to rely on the web site or email because his questions sometimes disappear into the blue and he never gets a response. This is unfortunate because he finds email more convenient than the phone.

Hillary, who wrote Note 2, is commenting on service times and reliability of information from your organisation. In the past she has been embarrassed when she has passed on the information that you have given to her, to her own customers. She has then had to let them down when your organisation has not been able to deliver on time.

Exercise 33

What does Bill need from your organisation?

....

What does Hillary need from your organisation?

....

Understanding customer needs

To give you some ideas, here are some examples of what customers might want from us - other than the service itself - when we provide a service to them.

Support

Help

Respect

Prompt attention

Empathy

A smile

Satisfaction

Additional help

To feel that the organisation cares

Courtesy

To be listened to

Regard for special needs

Resolution of problem or request

To be understood

Anticipation of needs

To be given the right service

Sensitivity to feelings

Exercise 34

Write down two more needs that a customer might have.

....

....

Exercise 35

Pick three of the needs listed on the previous page and give an example of what a customer who requests this means. We've done one for you as an example.

Courtesy   *Person helping me should say 'Good Morning' and be polite.*

....

....

....

It will help you to work out what customers want from you if you think about the times when YOU are a customer.

Exercise 36

Imagine that you went into a shop to buy a newspaper or a drink this morning.

Name four things that you would have liked to experience.

....

....

....

....

It's likely that you said something along the lines of:

• **Friendly service** – a friendly face goes down better than a grumpy one.

• **Prompt service** – we know that customers are served in turn but we don't want to be kept hanging around unnecessarily.

• **Polite service** – a 'please' and a 'thank you' will always be welcome.

• **Accurate service** – even if all the above three factors are present, if we arrive at our destination and find we have been given the wrong item then the transaction will have been a failure.

These are the **core customer needs** in most situations.

Extra needs

In addition to the basic needs that all customers are likely to have, as discussed above, some customers will have *extra* needs. Examples of customers who may have extra needs are:

- Customers with a *disability*

- Customers with *children*

- Customers who don't have a lot of *knowledge* about your services

- Customers who find it hard to *understand* you (eg because they don't speak English or are hard of hearing)

- Customers who find it hard to *communicate* their needs (eg because they have a speech defect)

- Customers from another *culture* who don't understand Australian customs

- Customers who are in a *hurry*

Assisting customers with extra needs

Imagine you are a parent with three grumpy children in tow, and you were compiling a list of your 'needs'. You might add "*Understanding*" and "*Additional help*" to the list of core needs that you created on page 61. Why?

- *Understanding* – because crying children are frustrating and perhaps embarrassing, so some empathy from others to show that they understand your situation would be welcome;

- *Additional help* – because if a member of staff could fetch the items you need or carry your basket or look after the oldest child or open a specially wide till area for you and your pushchair, your needs will be met much more efficiently.

Exercise 37

Give an example of how you might help the following customers who have 'extra needs'.

A customer who is hard of hearing and uses sign language and would like information on your services.

....

A tourist from Japan who is flummoxed by the range of coffees offered to him.

....

A father who would like to buy his daughter some clothes but doesn't know what to get.

....

An elderly lady who buys a large basketful of groceries but whose car is parked some distance away.

....

Enhancing the Quality of Your Service

To provide a top quality customer service you need to do more than just give customers what they have explicitly asked for. You should take every opportunity to set *your* organisation apart from others by offering an enhanced quality of service wherever possible. Consider the following situations.

- If a customer needs information from a bank on setting up a foreign currency account, then you must ensure that the *correct information* is given to him/her.

- If a customer comes into your shop and wants to buy children's clothing, you need to ensure s/he knows *where the children's clothing* is in your store and that s/he knows where the tills are.

- If a customer comes into your restaurant for a meal, you need to *take their order promptly*, serve their food efficiently and attend to their bill payment.

If you do the above, do you think you would have done a good job?

The answer is no. You will have done an *adequate* job, but there is much more that you could – and should – do to give the best possible service.

- In the first example, you could offer to set up an appointment for the customer with the foreign currency account manager so that any questions they have can be answered.

- In the second example, you could advise on style, size and make of clothes and on the differences between the various price ranges. If the customer has children with them, you might be able to arrange for some toys to be brought out to keep the children amused while the customer selects their purchases.

- In the third example, you should also attend to the customer's needs throughout the meal – checking whether they need any water or other drinks, etc. In 'recreational' activities such as dining, friendliness and courtesy are more important than ever – no one wants to eat their meal surrounded by grumpy waiting staff! In this way you can enhance the customer's dining experience and make him/her want to come back again.

Exercise 38

What could you do to exceed the customer's expectations in these situations?

1   A customer comes into your music shop and asks for a particular CD.

    You could point the customer towards the relevant aisle. What else could you do?

    ....

    ....

2   A customer asks for information on joining your gym.

    You could give the customer a price list. What else could you do?

    ....

    ....

The key is not just to live up to customers' expectations – but to EXCEED their expectations by giving them more than they thought they would receive. This sets your organisation apart from other organisations that offer a similar service to you.

Adding value to your service

The ideal time to impress customers with the quality of your service is while you are still serving them. While you have this contact you can 'add value' to the service by providing the customer with extra information and assistance. If you do this, your customer will regard your organisation as superior to other, similar, services because you will have exceeded their expectations regarding the service that they expected to receive.

Read through the following three conversations between Benny, the manager of the *On-time Secretarial Agency*, and a customer, Martha. You will see how Benny can add value to his service to help his customer better.

Conversation 1

Martha: Good morning. I'm faxing over five letters that I would like typed up please. I need to send them out tomorrow.

Benny: Thank you Martha. We will return those letters to you by the end of tomorrow, in time for you to catch the post. I look forward to speaking to you again when we may be of assistance to you.

Martha: Thank you Benny, goodbye.

Exercise 39

What impression do you think Martha would get of the On-time Secretarial Agency from this conversation? Write down your thoughts here.

....

....

....

Do you think Benny handled the call well?

....

....

....

It is likely, here, that Martha would think that Benny was friendly and helpful and that she would get her letters back in time to catch the post (although she may well be a bit pushed for time tomorrow afternoon to post the letters if she has a lot of other jobs to do).

Benny was polite and offered a service which he could deliver, but he didn't 'pull out the stops' for Martha or give Martha a better service than she might expect from any secretarial agency. Benny didn't give Martha any particular reason to return to the On-time Secretarial Agency next time she needs secretarial support.

Now consider another way Benny could have served Martha.

Conversation 2

Martha: Good morning. I'm faxing over five letters that I would like typed up please. I need to send them out tomorrow.

Benny: Thank you Martha. We will return those letters to you as soon as we can. I estimate that they will be with you by tomorrow lunchtime, so that you will have plenty of time to catch the post. If you would like us to type up your envelopes too, then just let me know. This may well save you some more time at your end. Is there anything else that I can help you with?

Martha: Not at the moment, thank you Benny, but I will call you next week as I know I am going to be busy them.

Benny: That's fine, Martha. I'll speak to you then. Goodbye.

Exercise 40

What do you think Martha would have thought of the On-time Secretarial Agency this time?

....

....

....

What do you think of Benny's service?

....

....

....

The author's thoughts

Here, Martha would be impressed that Benny was going to beat the deadline that she had given him by returning the letters by lunchtime rather than late in the afternoon. So he was going to give her as much extra time as he could. Martha would also be pleased that Benny had thoughtfully considered the fact that she might have a number of other tasks to perform tomorrow and had been proactive in thinking of other ways that his Agency could save her time and be of more assistance by suggesting typing up her envelopes.

Benny also asked if he could help Martha in any other way. This would have reassured Martha that Benny had time for her, appreciated her business and wanted to help.

Benny gave Martha a reason to come back to the On-time Secretarial Agency as she would know that Benny would offer a good service with extra services and improved turnaround times compared to other agencies.

Finally consider this conversation between Benny and Martha.

Conversation 3

Martha: Good morning. I'm faxing over five letters that I would like typed up please. I need to send them out tomorrow.

Benny: Thank you Martha. We will return those letters to you as soon as we can. I estimate that they will be with you by tomorrow lunchtime, so that you will have plenty of time to catch the post. If you would like us to type up your envelopes too, then just let me know. This may well save you some more time at your end.

You may be interested to know, Martha, that we also offer a posting service. We fax the typed letters over to you for approval, and then we put them in envelopes and take them to the Post Shop for you. This reduces your administration tasks substantially.

Martha: Mmm, I'm doing a large marketing mail-out in January. I'm sure that service will be helpful then.

Benny: Okay, I'll make a note in my diary to speak to you next week when you have more time. I can also send you a brochure which lists all of our services if that would be of interest to you?

Martha: Yes, I'd like to see that. I'll read it through and keep it for future reference.

Benny: Incidentally, can I ask if you know of anyone else who might be interested in seeing our brochure?

Martha: I'll give it some thought, I do know a couple of people who are looking for extra secretarial support during the holiday period. I'll let you know.

Benny: Thank you very much Martha. It was a pleasure speaking to you. I'll ensure your letters are back with you by lunchtime tomorrow and contact you next week about the mail-out. Is there anything else that I can help you with?

Martha: No thanks Benny. Goodbye.

Exercise 41

What do you think Martha would have made of this conversation?

....

....

....

What do you think of Benny's approach?

....

....

....

The author's thoughts

Martha would have been impressed with Benny's thoughtfulness and attention to detail as to how the On-time Secretarial Agency could help her with her needs. She was interested to hear about the services that Benny could offer which she hadn't previously been aware of and which would be helpful to her. Benny was proactive by guessing what services Martha might find helpful. By doing this – mentioning to Martha about the posting service the agency provides - he gains new business for the Agency.

Benny then found a way to inform Martha of all the different services that On-time offers – without delaying her on the telephone - by offering her a brochure. This will be informative and will also be a permanent physical reminder to Martha of the On-time Agency.

Finally, Benny worked on expanding his business by asking Martha if she had any contacts who might like to receive information on On-time. If Martha had been unwilling to pass on any names, Benny would have thanked her and moved on, but in this instance Martha was happy to give the matter some thought.

Note down three ways that a veterinary nurse could 'add value' when she is chatting to a lady who has brought her puppy in for its vaccinations. (Hint, can you think of other products or services that the customer may also be interested in?)

....

....

....

Further examples on enhancing the quality of service

In the example on the previous pages, involving the On-time Secretarial Agency, Benny enhanced the service he offered by:

- Exceeding Martha's service expectations by providing a faster service than requested

- Second guessing her needs

- Proactively suggesting further services that might assist her

- Asking if he could help her any further – giving her a chance to make comments or further enquiries. This makes a customer feel in control and valued

- Providing additional information in a useful format (a written brochure).

Here are some other examples of ways that quality of service can be enhanced.

Scenario 1: A furniture sales outlet

The customer requires a three-piece lounge suite to be delivered to his house the following weekend. The saleswoman, Jo, tells him that the suite will be delivered on Saturday.

How to enhance the delivery service: Jo could ask the customer which day – Saturday or Sunday – is more convenient to him and arrange for delivery to be made on that day. She could also give him a *time* for delivery rather than just a date. If this is not possible, Jo could try to arrange for the delivery people to phone the customer during the day on Saturday to give him a more accurate time for delivery.

Scenario 2: Internet beauty products service

The customer orders a bottle of perfume on-line and requests that it be sent to her mother on her birthday in one week's time. The company packages the perfume in bubble wrap and brown paper so that it will not break and posts the package so that it arrives in time for the birthday.

How to enhance the packaging service: The company could offer a gift-wrapping service for items that are to be sent as presents using patterned paper rather than plain brown paper. The company could also offer customers the chance to include a message with the gift. The company could offer 'Loyalty points' so that when a customer has spent a certain amount of money, they get a free gift or a discount on their next purchase.

Scenario 3: Computer repair centre

The customer takes her computer to a technician for repair. The technician, Lee, calls the customer one week later when the fault has been diagnosed and repaired, to let her know that the computer is ready to be collected.

How to enhance the repair service: As computers are integral to a lot of people's daily work, the technician could have checked whether the computer was needed back urgently. If it was, Lee could have offered a fast repair service (for extra cost, if appropriate). Lee should have phoned the customer more often to keep the customer informed of how the repairs were going – a daily phone call would probably be appropriate. Lee could also have offered to courier the computer back rather than requiring the customer to visit the repair centre again.

Scenario 4: Hotel

The hotel guest makes a number of complaints about the room that has been allocated to him, for example, he finds that the mini bar is empty, the trouser press is broken and the view is of the park rather than the beach, as he requested. The manager apologises and tells the guest that he will receive a reduction on his bill to compensate for these errors. When the guest leaves, the manager is not available and the bill is initially made up at the full rate. The assistant manager corrects this when the guest explains the situation.

How to enhance the service: The manager should have recorded the guest's complaints in writing at the time that they were made to ensure that the guest did not have to explain the situation again to a second person. The assistant manager should also have been kept informed (perhaps by way of a complaints register) of the compensation that the manager had offered to the guest to avoid confusion or argument.

Exercise 43

When problems occur in the course of delivering a service to customers, it is often useful to provide training so that the same problem does not occur again at a later date. It might be appropriate for training to be given to an individual or to a whole department.

Draw arrows to match up the training that would be appropriate in the situations listed on the left.

Problem situation	*Training*
Joyce doesn't return two customers' phone calls because she doesn't know how to access their account details on the computer network.	*Ordering procedures*
Jason doesn't record payments made by customers correctly, resulting in customers being sent late payment reminders when they had actually paid their account in full.	*Time management*
Jenny misses two deadlines for sending business documents to clients because she concentrated on completing non-urgent matters first.	*Accounting procedures*
Jerry doesn't take down all the details of products required by a customer, resulting in dispatch of the goods being delayed.	*In-house Computer systems*

Handling Complaints

Just because a customer or client has a complaint doesn't mean that the situation is destined to turn out badly. With skilful handling you can leave the customer feeling very good about your company or organisation – perhaps better than they felt before the problem cropped up.

Consider your own experience. Have you ever been back to a shop to return faulty goods feeling that you didn't want to shop there again because of the inconvenience?

- If the shop assistant listened to your complaint and dealt with it well, the chances are that you have gone back.

BEFORE

- If nobody wanted to know and dismissed your problem without considering it properly – you probably haven't ever gone back.

Complaints are an important communication channel, and they enable you to improve your service. If customers complain, at least you have been given a chance to put things right.

How not to deal with a complaint

Example 1

A customer complains to a catering company, which had provided the buffet lunch at a conference she organised. She leaves a message on the catering company's answer machine saying that there was insufficient food to cover the number of attendees and the sandwiches were stale. Therefore she would like the invoice reduced.

The catering company doesn't return the phone call and reissues the invoice for the same amount. They send her a letter commenting on her late payment. The company thinks that the customer probably invited more people to the conference than she had planned to, and that must have been the reason there was too little food.

Example 2

A customer complains to a house cleaning agency saying that she has found muddy footprints all over her carpet and thick dirt in the oven.

The agency says that cleaning ovens was never in the contract and if the client had wanted her oven cleaned she should have said so when she engaged them. They aren't mind-readers after all, they say. As for muddy footprints – they tell the customer that she had better check her own shoes as the prints are more likely to be her own than their cleaners' footprints.

Even though we don't know the full facts in either of these situations, we can still tell that the way these organisations have dealt with the problems is not appropriate. Whose <u>fault</u> a problem is, is not the most important matter. Resolving the problem <u>is</u>.

Exercise 44

Write down how you think the organisations in the two examples on the previous page could have handled the situation better.

Example 1: ....

....

....

Example 2: ....

....

....

How do complaints arise?

Complaints can arise in all sorts of situations. Sometimes they can be attributed to being someone's fault but sometimes not. In most situations, finding out who is to blame should come second to remedying the situation. It is usually, however, appropriate *after* you have satisfied the customer, to find out where the problem arose and take steps to ensure that it doesn't happen again.

Here are some examples of problems that customers may complain about.

© Software Educational Resources Ltd

Exercise 45

Write down an example of a complaint that an external customer might have in the following workplaces.

1 Petrol station

   ....

2 Airport

   ....

3 Car repair shop

   ....

4 Travel agency

   ....

5 Dental practice

   ....

The basics in dealing with complaints

➢ Remember that the customer is not complaining about you – it is the situation so don't take it personally.

➢ See the positive side - handled properly you can make a customer yours for life.

➢ Be polite and keep calm. If the customer is angry, getting angry back won't help.

➢ Show empathy, eg say, *"I am sorry you have cause for complaint"* – and encourage the customer to start explaining rather than just complaining.

➢ Don't try to apportion fault or blame.

Listen and gather information

➢ Let the customer have his/her say.

➢ Remember that a person with a complaint is upset and will often exaggerate.

➢ Guide the customer into telling you about the problem by asking questions.

➢ Take written notes. This shows sincerity and gives you the information you need to take the right action.

➢ Don't agree or disagree with the complaint until you have all the information you need. For example, don't say "Yes, I agree it shouldn't do that" before you have heard the full story. You may get your company into trouble by offering your own opinion too soon as the customer may use your opinion to try and get their own way.

Exercise 46

Rate the following comments to a complaining customer on a scale of 1 to 5, with 1 being 'Very good' and 5 being 'Very poor'.

Scenario: The customer ordered furniture for delivery to her home address. She wrote her details on the appropriate form but admits that she didn't use very neat handwriting. She has waited in all day but the furniture hasn't arrived.

"Now, hold on a moment, this is your fault remember - you must have written down the wrong address for delivery, no wonder it's got lost."	1	2	3	4	5
"I'm sorry to hear you are still waiting. I will call the driver on his mobile phone and find out what is happening. Would you mind holding the line?"	1	2	3	4	5
"That's no good. We shouldn't be keeping you waiting. I'll give the driver a call when I get a chance."	1	2	3	4	5
"You've been waiting HOW LONG?! You must be furious."	1	2	3	4	5

Interpersonal skills

It is in difficult situations such as when customers complain, that your interpersonal skills will be vital. Look back to the interpersonal skills section in this book.

Three skills that will be particularly appropriate are:

➢ Mature judgement

➢ Tact

➢ Discretion

Exercise 47

Write down how each of these three skills could be helpful when dealing with customers with complaints.

Mature judgement

....

....

Tact

....

....

Discretion

....

....

Responding to the customer

Can you fix the problem?

You must know company policy.

What if you can't fix the problem?

You should hand the complaint to more experienced staff. Give the staff member who is to deal with the complaint all the information that you have. Don't make the customer repeat their story all over again.

AFTER

Keep the customer informed

Tell the customer what you are doing.

Be prompt

Let the customer know when someone will get back to them and make it soon – time that they spend waiting for resolution of their complaint is time they spend potentially having a bad opinion of your company. Complaints can be difficult and even unpleasant situations, but don't make that an excuse to delay – the complaint won't go away and can only get worse.

Does the complaint need more investigation?

If so, explain this. Tell the customer you will report back by a certain time - and make sure you do.

What action does the customer want?

Often the customer just needs to blow off steam. If there is genuine cause for complaint then the customer's annoyance is justified. Ask the customer what he/she expects - it could be that all they want is for their complaint to be recorded.

If the company is not at fault, make sure you explain this. You will need to draw on all your communication skills and be very tactful. An angry customer does not like to be told they are in the wrong.

Remedying problems

Every organisation is different so it is impossible to give detailed advice on how complaints can be remedied. However, the following general guidelines will be helpful. Remember that your own organisation's rules and procedures will take precedence over those detailed here, where they vary.

Damaged goods

Information you need to find out

Is the damage fundamental to the operation of the product or just cosmetic. Was the damage evident when the goods were purchased? Was the damage caused by inappropriate use of the goods? Were the goods sold at a reduced price due to the damage?

Remedy

Can you give a refund or exchange the goods? If not, can you advise the customer how to avoid the same problem occurring again. Can you give the customer a discount if they have to buy the product again?

Undelivered goods

Information you need to find out

Do you have the correct address details for the customer? Have the correct details been given to the delivery department? Does the customer have the correct delivery date and time details? Do you know where the goods are? Can you trace the goods? Have the goods left your warehouse yet? Has the driver been delayed rather than omitting to deliver the goods? Were the goods sent by registered post?

Remedy

Ensure you have correct delivery address details. Arrange re-delivery as soon as possible. If possible and appropriate, give the customer a reduction on the delivery cost to off-set the inconvenience. If possible, give the customer a time for delivery (rather than just a date) to reduce further inconvenience.

An administrative error, such as an incorrect invoice issued or goods charged for at the wrong price

Information you need to find out

Which departments in your organisation need to know about this error in order for records to be amended (eg the accounting department)? Do you have authority to amend such documents? Is the document definitely incorrect – check with manager/supervisor/other colleagues in your department that the price given wasn't quoted for a special reason.

Remedy

Arrange for reissue of any erroneous documents. If applicable, advise customer of steps taken in-house to ensure such errors don't reoccur.

A warehouse or store room error, such as the incorrect product delivered

Information you need to find out

Which departments in your organisation need to know about this error in order for records to be amended (eg purchasing department or accounts department)? Was the correct product ordered by the customer – and therefore invoiced for or will invoices need to be amended too.

Remedy

Arrange re-delivery as soon as possible – is courier delivery an option? If appropriate, give the customer a reduction on the delivery cost to off-set the inconvenience. If possible, give the customer a time for delivery (rather than just a date) to reduce the amount of further inconvenience. Arrange for reissue of any erroneous documents. If applicable, advise customer of steps taken in-house to ensure such errors don't reoccur.

A service error, such as an appliance not repaired properly or a service performed badly

Information you need to find out

Obtain exact details of error complained of. Should the aspect of the service complained of have been provided (eg if customer complains that paint on car being serviced wasn't touched up – would the paint normally be touched up during that service?). If customer is complaining about the price, was a quote given first? Were all paperwork and authorising documents completed by the customer beforehand?

Remedy

If applicable, can the appliance (for example) still be repaired under warranty. Ensure customer knows of any extra charges that may be incurred if service technicians do further work and discover that the problem was caused by customer error. If appropriate, re-perform the service free of charge. If that is not appropriate, can a reduction or other benefit be given to the customer.

Customer dissatisfied with the service even though it is performed adequately, eg they don't like their new hair colour, even though they requested it and it was applied correctly

Information you need to find out

Did the customer explain exactly what they wanted? Did they get what they asked for? Is the situation reversible, eg can a service acceptable to the customer still be given?

Remedy

Correct the service if possible (eg a new hair colour could be applied). If appropriate, supply extra services at a reduced cost to reverse what has been done.

Exercise 48

The following are poor responses to complaints from customers. Suggest a better way of responding below.

At the Pet Shop

Customer: I bought this rabbit hutch last week but the wood seems to be split. Can I have my money back?

Shop assistant: You were probably very rough with it. Nobody else has had a problem with that hutch.

Your suggested response:

....

....

....

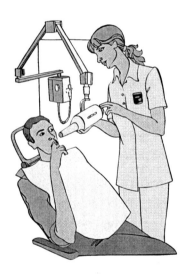

At the Dentist

Client: I've been waiting in the waiting room for the dentist for an hour now and people that have come in after me have gone in before me. I want to go in next.

Receptionist: Your name isn't on the list, you obviously didn't register with me properly. You'll have to wait your turn.

Your suggested response:

....

....

....

Difficult Situations and Problem Customers

While we might wish that all customers would be a pleasure to deal with at all times (as we ourselves aim to be!), it is very likely that at some stage you will come across some difficult situations, for example a customer may be angry, upset, won't stop talking, etc. You should learn to handle these customers so that you can deal with them quickly and effectively. Take note of the following 'problem' customers and suggestions for dealing with them.

- **The indecisive customer**

If the customer has difficulty deciding what they want from you, you should use your effective questioning skills to ascertain what their requirements are and then help them come to a satisfactory decision. Use open questions to help the customer express their thoughts. Give information on the various products or services that are available that fit their requirements and explain the differences between the various products and services to help them decide between them.

- **The upset customer**

An upset customer will often exaggerate. You should be calm and sympathetic and use your questioning skills to encourage the customer to discuss the issue with you. When he/she is calmer, you can suggest ways that their problem could be addressed. Ensure that the customer agrees with your recommended solution and don't bulldoze them into agreement. If you do not have the authority to solve the problem, contact the relevant member of staff and explain the issue to them. Double-check that the staff member attends to the problem.

- **The chatty customer**

There are customers who seem to be more interested in having a chat, than explaining their enquiry. This can waste time both for the customer and you. In this case, you should steer the conversation to the service required, and conclude the conversation politely. Focus on the service rather than having a more general discussion. Don't allow the conversation to deviate. Use closed questions to keep the customer on track. Be careful not to appear rude by rushing the customer.

- **The angry customer**

Be polite and keep calm because getting angry too won't help matters. Ask the customer questions and encourage them to tell you what they are angry about. Don't agree or apologise until you have all the information you need to be able to make a decision on the problem. If you cannot deal with the customer yourself, refer him or her to a person with the authority to resolve the matter as promptly as possible.

- **The complaining customer**

Show empathy (eg say, "I am sorry you have cause for complaint"). Let the customer have his/her say and guide him/her into telling you about the problem by asking questions. Take written notes as this shows sincerity and gives you the information you need to take the right action. Don't agree or disagree with the complaint until you have all the information you need. Check company policy before taking action. If you cannot deal with the complaint yourself, refer it to the person with the authority to resolve the matter as promptly as possible.

Feedback

After you have completed serving the customer, it is very useful to gain feedback from the customer regarding:

➢ what they liked about the service

➢ how they thought the service could be improved.

Feedback from customers is invaluable, as you can try and imagine what customers think about your organisation and your services, but your customers are the only ones that can actually tell you for *certain*.

Ways to get feedback, include

➢ asking the customer personally

➢ customer focus groups

➢ questionnaires (you often find these in hotel rooms, restaurants and at training centres)

➢ suggestion boxes

➢ recording of complaints.

Talking to the customer is very useful, but you may find that customers are more reluctant to discuss the negative feelings that they have about your organisation and its services.

Questionnaires and suggestions boxes are anonymous and therefore you may get a more honest view from these.

Don't let negative feedback get you down – it is good that your customers are telling you. This means that you have a chance to put the negative things right and improve your service.

Learn from your experiences

The most important thing is to learn from your experiences and from the information that you gather. There is no point in having a suggestion box which is never emptied, or a pile of completed questionnaires that no one bothers to read.

Consider all comments and ask yourself:

➢ Was that customer happy?

➢ If not, why did a problem occur?

➢ What can I do to avoid that problem occurring again?

➢ If that problem was to happen again, could I handle it better?

Exercise 49

Imagine that you received the following note in a suggestion box at the electronic appliance repair shop you work at.

> My vacuum cleaner was repaired but I wasn't told that there would be a charge to cover the time you initially spent looking over the cleaner. I thought all charges would be covered by the warranty. I found that a bit annoying. Plus it seems to have a lot more scratches on it than it did when I brought it in. Incidentally, do you sell second-hand machines? I would be interested in a food processor.
>
> Carol

Make a note of what areas of your business you need to look at to ensure that these problems don't occur again.

....

....

....

What extra steps could you put in place to enhance your service based on the comments in this note.

....

....

....

....

Summary

1   Be polite - remember to thank the customer.

2   Be clear – ensure that the customer knows what to expect from your service (this will reduce the chance of any misunderstandings leading to complaints later).

3   Be helpful - ask if there is anything else that you can do for the customer – this may jog their memory if they need any further help from you.

4   Add value and proactively improve the quality of your service where possible - you will impress the customer and may obtain further business.

5   Get feedback.

6   Act on feedback gained and learn from your experiences.

Exercise 50

Imagine that you work at a kindergarten looking after toddlers from 11.00 am to 1.00 pm each weekday. Today a new customer, Mrs Mathis, is bringing her son, Ben, to kindergarten. Following the six steps listed above, make notes here on how you would treat Mrs Mathis and Ben on their first day at your kindergarten. The first one has been done for you.

Step 1: Politeness Welcome Mrs Mathis and Ben. Introduce them to other parents and children. Show them around the kindergarten.

Step 2: Clarity ....

....

Step 3: Helpfulness ....

....

Step 4: Add value ....

....

Step 5: Get feedback ....

....

Step 6: Act on feedback ....

....

Notes

Revision

1   Explain the following types of customer.

    External: ....

    Internal: ....

    Agency: ....

2   Name three active listening techniques.

    ....

    ....

    ....

3   Give two examples of factors that might affect a customer's choice when buying a product or service.

    a   ....

    b   ....

4   When should you refer a customer to another person rather than helping them yourself?

    ....

5   List two documents that may provide information about your organisation's requirements on how customers should be treated.

    a   ....

    b   ....

6   Explain why you need to prioritise customer needs.

    ....

    ....

7   Explain very briefly how you might deal with the following customers.

    A complaining customer: ....

    ....

    An indecisive customer: ....

    ....

© Software Educational Resources Ltd

Skills Test

Imagine that you work at the Lakeside Conference Centre. Various functions take place there, including weddings, training courses, seminars and conferences. You deal directly with clients who wish to hold functions at the Lakeside Conference Centre to ensure that they are provided with everything they need while they are at Lakeside.

1   List two external customers and two internal customers who you would deal with in your role.

    External (a) ....

              (b) ....

    Internal (a) ....

            (b) ....

2   The managing director of a company based in a large city about 40 kilometres away makes an appointment to visit you, as she is interested in holding a sales conference at Lakeside. Note down some steps that you will take to put your customer at ease when she arrives and to help establish a good rapport with her.

    ....

    ....

    ....

3   You return from lunch to find the following messages have been left for you. Place them into order of priority:

    (A) "The bride who is having a wedding here on Sunday rang to ask about floral decorations. Please give her a call."

    (B) "The manager of the *Cicero Group Training Centre* rang. His training rooms are flooded and he needs somewhere to hold a course tomorrow morning. Do you have a room available?"

    (C) "The clients in room 12 would like to use the overhead projector this afternoon. Please set it up for them."

    (D) "The secretary of the company which held their board meeting in the Gallery Room yesterday would like to talk to you about holding next month's board meeting here too. Please ring them."

    Order of priority: ....

4   When you are chatting to the receptionist, Lili, one day about future bookings, Lili tells you that she is so busy that when customers come in, she carries on working on the computer while sorting out their query in order to save time. You notice also that when she is talking to customers she often walks away from the customer towards your office in order to get queries answered. You need to have a talk with her about body language and what signals she is sending to customers by her actions. Jot down some points you want to cover in your conversation with Lili.

....

....

....

5   Jim, a local baker, wants to hold an event at the Lakeside. He is not very clear – and seems a little confused - about the details. Read through what Jim tells you. Then list three questions that you would ask Jim to help you understand what facilities he will need.

Jim: "It's going to be huge. All the bakers in our district and some others probably. We're going to have a presentation, with all the bells and whistles. Not just a speech – much more high tech than that. Obviously the food has got to be up to scratch – what with us being bakers. We could have tea and cakes - or maybe steak and chips. I wonder which would be best. It's a one-day conference. We'll come on the Wednesday and probably spend the weekend here. Everyone will need single rooms and spouses might be invited too. It's going to be great!"

Your questions:

....

....

....

6   The Lakeside has four settings where wedding receptions are normally held: the botanical gardens, a large ballroom, the restaurant and bar area, and the pretty tea-rooms. Based on their comments below, match the most appropriate setting to four couples:

Couple 1: We want a proper sit down evening meal in a formal setting with waiters so that our guests can relax.

Suggested setting: _____

Couple 2: We are inviting lots of people of all ages – there'll be lots of children so it would be good to have space for them to run around. We want a really pretty, informal setting with nibbles and finger food brought to us as we wander about chatting to people.

Suggested setting: _____

Couple 3: We are having a small, morning wedding. We'd like our guests to be able to have morning coffee and cakes. We'd like it to be relaxed but our guests (and us!) are in our fifties, so we don't want it to be too wild!

Suggested setting: _____

Couple 4: We'd like a disco that goes on well into the early hours. The weather doesn't look too good so we'd like to be indoors and have a buffet – with loads of food available throughout the evening for guests to have when they feel hungry.

Suggested setting: _____

© Software Educational Resources Ltd

7 Unfortunately, a customer who held a seminar at the Lakeside last month has written to you with some complaints. Read through his letter and make some notes about how you will respond. Also make some notes about how you might avoid these problems occurring again.

"We enjoyed our event at the Lakeside generally speaking, however I do have a few complaints. At dinner, we were given a table for eight people, but there were ten of us so it was very embarrassing. I know that I originally told you there would be eight people, but I did ring the day before to tell you numbers had gone up. I left you a message but you obviously didn't get it.

It was particularly frustrating because when I asked the waiter to move an empty table next to us to accommodate the extra people, he said that the receptionist had the list of bookings for the evening and he wasn't allowed to move the furniture around in case the tables were booked!

Also, the overhead projector that you gave us wasn't one I'm familiar with and when I needed some help in making it work I was told that no one at Lakeside knew how to work it either as it had only just been bought.

I must say the room and its view were superb though. I look forward to your comments.

Keith Parker."

8 One morning, you receive three telephone calls. Note down whether you would be able to deal with the calls yourself or whether you need to refer the caller to another member of staff. If so, who?

Caller 1: "I'm looking for bed and breakfast accommodation for three nights in July. Can you help?"

Deal with or refer (if so, who to): _____

Caller 2: "I am a student looking for work over the summer period. Do you have any vacancies for housemaiding staff?"

Deal with or refer (if so, who to): _____

Caller 3: "I'm having a conference in March and am looking for a friendly, efficient facility to have it in that can accommodate various needs."

Deal with or refer (if so, who to): _____

Revision Answers

Revision Answers

1	**Explain the following types of customer.**
	External: "Out of house" – they come from a different organisation.
	Internal: "In-house" – colleagues from within the same organisation.
	Agency: Groups and other organisations, rather than the individuals that work within them.
2	**Name three active listening techniques.**
	Encouraging, rephrasing and summarising.
3	**Give two examples of factors that might affect a customer's choice when buying a product or service.**
	a) Shelf life b) Features
4	**When should you refer a customer to another person rather than helping them yourself?**
	When the customer's enquiry is outside your area of knowledge or authority.
5	**List two documents that may provide information about your organisation's requirements on how customers should be treated.**
	Job description, Workplace manual.
6	**Explain why you need to prioritise customer needs.**
	To ensure that the service you deliver to customers is provided within the appropriate timeframe and meets any deadlines that the customer has told you about.
7	**Explain very briefly how you might deal with the following customers.**
	A complaining customer: Show empathy. Let the customer explain the problem – encourage this by asking questions. Make sure you have all the relevant information. Check company policy before taking action. Refer the customer to another member of staff if the complaint is outside your area of authority.
	An indecisive customer: Ask open questions to help them decide what they need the product or service for and to explain what their requirements are. Explain the different products or services and discuss various factors, such as the price, features, maintenance, etc, to help the customer make their final choice.